Young Writers 2005 PO

PLAYground POets

Let your creativity flow...

ode

limerick   haiku

rhyme

- Inspirations From The West Country

Edited by Steve Twelvetree

 Young**Writers**

First published in Great Britain in 2005 by:
Young Writers
Remus House
Coltsfoot Drive
Peterborough
PE2 9JX
Telephone: 01733 890066
Website: www.youngwriters.co.uk

SB ISBN 1 84602 274 6

Foreword

Young Writers was established in 1991 and has been passionately devoted to the promotion of reading and writing in children and young adults ever since. The quest continues today. Young Writers remains as committed to the fostering of burgeoning poetic and literary talent as ever.

This year's Young Writers competition has proven as vibrant and dynamic as ever and we are delighted to present a showcase of the best poetry from across the UK. Each poem has been carefully selected from a wealth of *Playground Poets* entries before ultimately being published in this, our thirteenth primary school poetry series.

Once again, we have been supremely impressed by the overall high quality of the entries we have received. The imagination, energy and creativity which has gone into each young writer's entry made choosing the best poems a challenging and often difficult but ultimately hugely rewarding task - the general high standard of the work submitted amply vindicating this opportunity to bring their poetry to a larger appreciative audience.

We sincerely hope you are pleased with our final selection and that you will enjoy *Playground Poets - Inspirations From The West Country* for many years to come.

Contents

Bishops Cannings CE Primary School, Devizes

Jack Langham (10)	17
Matthew Woods (11)	17
Elysia Walker (9)	18
Amy Holt (8)	18
Serran Aziz (11)	19
Jack Braine (11)	19
Amber Linsley (11)	20
Sophie Hay (8)	20
Laura Drew (7)	20
Sarah Carroll (8)	21
Charlotte Little (11)	21
Rachel Holt (7)	21
Oliver Hector (10)	22
Emily Wellbelove (11)	23
Jordan Hicks (11)	23
Tansy Dando (11)	24
Ruby Francis (11)	25
Drew Kewley (11)	25
Jake Grover (11)	26
George Dunford (11)	26
Lauren Hookings (11)	27
Matthew Lever (11)	27
Bethan Lightowler (10)	28
Milan Johnson (10)	28
Michael Wall (9)	28
Sarah Jane Hunt (8)	29
Oliver Powlesland (11)	29
Abbie Coleman (8)	29
Hannah Weston (11)	30

Forest & Sandridge CE Primary School, Melksham

Adam Watson (9)	30
Rhys Dunn (10)	31
Candice Walters (7)	31
Henry Meakin (10)	31
Karis Simmons (8)	32
Samantha Purves (8)	32
Hannah Webb (7)	33
Laura Park (9)	33
Rachel McNally (8)	34

Molly Adams (7)	34
Katie Gulliford (9)	35
Thomas Clover (8)	35
Courtney Bridger (9)	35
Eleana Murphy (7)	36

Headley Park Primary School, Bristol

Owen Burnell (8)	36
Ashleigh Britton (9)	37
Amy Ward (9)	37
Henry Harper (9)	38
Harry Browning (9)	38
Jonathan Searle (9)	39
Liam Norris (8)	39
Jake Burston (9)	40
Josie Cameron (8)	40
Molly Quantick (8)	41
Georgia Elson (7)	41
Matthew Hawkins (9)	42
Abigail Pratten (9)	42
Charlotte Williams (9)	43
Jesse Payne (8)	43
Megan Pope (9)	44
Kimberley Sargent (9)	44
Jessie Carey (8)	45
George Hancock (7)	45
Wesley Lewis Williams (8)	46
Jennifer Taylor (8)	46

Horrington Primary School, Wells

Harriet Seymour (9)	47
Angus Morrice (9)	47
George Hill (8)	48
Emma Keene (7)	48
Grace James (9)	49
Ellie Massey (7)	49
Jamie Tweed (8)	50
Freyja Chitty	50
Isaac Stone (8)	50
Nancy Lunnon (8)	51
Hayley Withers (9)	51

Josh Cook (8)   52
Ellie Oliva-Knight (8)   52
Rosie Davies (8)   52
Anna Williams (9)   53
Danielle Hill (8)   53
Luke Jenkins (9)   54

Kingsmoor Primary School, Bridgwater

Gregory Chapman (11)   54
Ross Bowden (11)   55
Phoebe Fisher (11)   56
Jonathan Hill (11)   57
Ben Judge (11)   58
Sam Biddulph (10)   59
Nathan Creedy (11)   60
Sarah Parsons (11)   61
Gabriella Robinson (11)   62
Emily Clyne (11)   62
Victoria Elizabeth Chapman (11)   63
Ffion Jones (11)   64
Sophie Thyer (11)   65
Emily Easman (11)   66
Nicholas Hughes (10)   67
Nathan Bale (11)   68
Robert House (11)   69
Jack Plummer (10)   70
Scott Chidgey (9)   71
Michael Watts (10)   72
Bradley Quint (10)   73
Marie Gibbs (10)   74
Christopher McMinn (10)   75
Lucy Kate Williams (10)   76
Stephanie Nicole Elkins (11)   77
Timothy Walker (10)   78

Kingston St Mary CE Primary School, Taunton

Bertie Adam, Leanna Bond (11) & Rosie Jenord (10)   78
Amy Hunter (8)   79
Holly Salter (9)   79
George Clews & Jack Sweet (9)   80
Helena Minnis (9)   80

Kirsten Hancock (9)	81
Molly Durrant (9)	81
Sam Preston (9)	81
Kathryn Littlewood (9)	82

La Retraite Swan School, Salisbury

Charlotte Jones (11)	82
Christiana Berezin (8)	82
Oliver Bradshaw (10)	83
William Bailey-Hobbs (8)	83
James Cole	84
Imogen Blair (10)	85
Robin Sedden (9)	85
Lydia Edwards (11)	86
Alice Pearse (9)	86
Kathryn Hoddinott (11)	86
Sophie Forster (11)	87
Elina Ho (8)	87
Lucy Robson (11)	88
Nia Singleton (11)	88
Eva Bryan (9)	89
Georgina Dollittle (10)	89
Charlotte Nicol (11)	90
Kirsty Ballard (11)	90
Hannah Webber (10)	91
Chloe Fooks (11)	91
William Sharpe (10)	92
Georgia Edwards (8)	92
Catherine Morrison (10)	93
Jack Killick (9)	93
Hugh McLean (10)	94
Molly Cook (11)	94
Caroline Attard (9)	95
Alice Bowen (9)	95
Jessica Webber (9)	96
Stephanie Davey (10)	96
Nicholas Finlayson (10)	97
William Garston (9)	97
Chloe David (10)	98
James Bold (9)	98
Molly Viner (10)	99

Emma Peacey (10)	99
Jordan Griffiths (10)	100
Lindsey Budd (10)	100
Patrick Ba-Tin (10)	101
Victoria Davey (8)	101
Jordan Neale (10)	102
Laura Hollingbery (9)	102
Elizabeth Morgan (9)	103
Olivia Wilson (10)	103
Clive Marcus (11)	104
James Martin (10)	104
Theo Daniel (10)	105
George Sharpe (9)	106
William Hoddinott (9)	106
Oscar Treleaven (9)	107
Harry Hart (9)	107

Longwell Green Primary School, Bristol

Spencer Ford (9)	107
Jacob Miller (9)	108
Jessica Dudley (10)	108
Aaron Gough (9)	108
Yasmin Shirmanesh (9)	109
Hannah Tapscott (8)	109
Joshua Munday (9)	109
Corey Reid (9)	109
Rachel Lim (8)	110
Charlotte Hawley (9)	110
Isabel Daone (9)	110
Anna Clark (9)	110
Daniel Davies (9)	111
Jack Williams (8)	111
Joshua Collins (8)	111
Shannon Ponter (9)	111
Ben Clapp (9)	112
Thomas George (9)	112
Jason Granville (8)	112
Ella Hicken (8)	112
Lucy Gazzard (9)	113
Mitchell Thornton (9)	113
Elliott Gibbons (9)	113

Lydeard St Lawrence School, Taunton

Hannah Adams (10)	114
Rebecca Down (9)	114
William McColl (9)	115
Daniel Sinkins (10)	115
Josh Newman (11)	116
Drummond Kesson Ross (10)	117
Alice Baldwin	118
Laurence Ryan (10)	119
Patrick Greenway (9)	120
Megan Morley (10)	121
Elly Greenway (11)	122
Aidan R Johnson (10)	122
Tansy Purdey (10)	123
Rhys Walker (9)	123
Guy Penny (9)	124
Robert Gribble (11)	124
Sarah Spiller (10)	125
Samantha Gridley (10)	125
Alice Baker (11)	126
James Goodman (11)	126

Mead Vale Primary School, Weston-super-Mare

Hannah Price (10)	127
Stefan Richards (11)	128
Benjamin Gutsell (11)	129
Eleanor Tunnicliffe (10)	129
Joshua Smart (10)	130
Sam Casey (11)	130
Olivia Sandys (9)	131
Charlotte Balcombe (10)	131
Sophie Bishop-Hurman (11)	132
Joe Edwards (10)	132
Stephanie Clark (10)	132
Amber Morris (11)	133
Curtis Dowdell (11)	133
Jordan Puddy (10)	133
Jessica Durant (11)	134
Lucy Dennis (10)	134

Overndale School, Bristol

Matthew Harvey (8)	135
Jack Harris (8)	136
Katie Bennett (8)	137
Kerry-Dee Shaw (10)	138
Francesca Causon (10)	139
Maddie Hopkinson-Buss (9)	140
Lawrence Luffman (9)	141

Ramsbury Primary School, Marlborough

Nicola Pope (11)	141
Sophie Scott (10)	142
Andrew Bethwaite (11)	143
Charlie Butler (11)	144
Jessica Dixon (11)	144
Emily Hertzell (10)	145
Francesca Barrett (11)	145
Sam Chapman (11)	146
Jack Smith (10)	146
David Reynolds (11)	146
Leo Dennis (11)	147
Gary Hall (11)	147
Harry Field (11)	147
Hattie Clark (11)	148
Grace Harker (11)	148
Lizzie Wilson (10)	148
Daniel Jones (10)	149
Harry Swain (11)	149
Rebecca Court (10)	149
Archie Bhatt-Monro (11)	150
Harry Fisher (11)	150
Jacob Clay (10)	151

St Benedict's RC School, Midsomer Norton

Katie Eastman (9)	151
Jamilla Griffin (9)	152
Haiden Albrow (9)	152
Ellie Gilkerson (9)	152
Hannah Silkstone (9)	153
Samantha Mitchell (9)	153
Emily Moon (8)	154

Lonneke Kertzman (9)	154
Gavin Vincent S Phillips (9)	154
Tom Meddings (9)	155
Verity Rose Hallett (9)	155
Katie Fletcher (9)	155
Connor Riddle (8)	156
Kris-Mae Dela Isla (9)	156
William Hunt (11)	157
Charlie Frost (9)	157
Radika McCarthy-Singh (10)	158
Westly Frood (9)	158
Toby Frayling (9)	159

St Bernard's School, Bristol

Olan Kenny (8)	159
Ornella Navari (9)	160
Krystie-Annah Hooper (9)	160
Lewis Barker-Muzzell (9)	161
Ashley Harrison (8)	161
Ella Calland (8)	161
Rosie Shaughnessy (9)	162
Tom Jewell (9)	162
Liam Hawkins (9)	162
Molly Phillips (9)	163
Kyle Nolan (9)	163

Sambourne Primary School, Warminster

Helen Hulbert (10)	163
Rhys Jones (10)	164
Brandon South (10)	164
Charlotte McDermott (11)	165
Jonathan Skinner (11)	165
Oliver Nash (10)	166
Ryan Hudd (10)	166
Sophie Skinner (10)	167
Bethany Usher (10)	167
Jamie Denton (10)	168
Michael Gemine (10)	168
Stephen Mathews (10)	169
Sam Clift (10)	169
Rhiannan Player (10)	170

Mark Dennis Burton (10)   170
Katy Ford (10)   170
Jade Pinnell (10)   171
Ben Jeanes (10)   171
George Hartnell (11)   172
Elizabeth Johnston (10)   172
Ben Phelps (10)   172
Thomas Redding (11)   173
Kirsty Wheeler (11)   173
Hannah Collett (10)   174
Nicola Mousley (11)   174
Shaun Marlow (11)   175

Shirehampton Junior School, Bristol
Jorden Kenyon & Paige Williams (11)   175
Aaron Harvey & Luke Carey (9)   176
Yacine Nouq, Joe Carter & Joe Golder   176
Tara Louise Dixon (10)   177
Katie Ackerman, Laura Jones & Amy West (9)   177
Danielle Hodges (9)   178

Shrewton Primary School, Salisbury
Kimberley Chapman (11)   178
Emma Palmer (11)   179
Jane Brown (11)   179
Ellie Selby (11)   180
Joe Johns (10)   180
Lauren Harwood (10)   181

Sutton Veny CE Primary School, Warminster
Nicole Esdaile (10)   181
Max Betteridge (11)   182
Alexander Mitchell (11)   182
Jeremy Smith (11)   182
Bianca Wolkenstein (11)   183
Rebecca Young (10)   183
Benjamin Dews (10)   183
Lee Cooper (11)   184
Becky Prior (11)   184
Fergus Frank (10)   184
Henry John (10)   185

Cameron Halkett (11)	185
Seth Roberts (10)	185
Jennifer Irons (10)	186
Lauren McComish (10)	186
Lucy Waters (11)	186
Zöe Fitzgerald (11)	187
Katie Lampard (11)	187
Louis McBride (10)	187
Rosie Hall (11)	188
Ben Winter (11)	188
Rebecca Freestone (10)	189

The Tynings CP School, Bristol

Ollie Harper-Bill (9)	189
Emily McCoy (10)	189
George Jefferies (10)	190
Alice Wood (10)	190
Nic Shore (10)	190
Shaun Flook (10)	191
Calum McDonald (10)	191
Daniel McCarthy (10)	192
Rowan James (10)	192
Jacob Wiltshire (10)	193
Jodie Britton (10)	193
Hope Bowyer (10)	194
Eleanor Sheppard (10)	195
Victoria Wright (10)	196
Sam Evans (10)	197
Rebecca Walsh (10)	198
Lauren Handford (10)	198
Callum Flett (9)	199

Wanborough Primary School, Swindon

Alice Nugent (9)	199
Alice Roberts (10)	200
Olivia Tuck (8)	200
Katie Pullan (10)	201
Alex Babington (8)	201
Daniel Waldron (9)	202
Jessica Ridler (9)	202
Megan Paper (10)	203

Olivia Witts (8)	203
Jonathon Nicholls (9)	204
Hannah Mills (9)	204
Daniel Thomas (10)	205
Bradley Mitchell (9)	205
Ben White (10)	206
Jack Mason (10)	206
Bethany Meaden (10)	207
Megan Street (10)	207
Callum Egan (10)	208
Oliver Berwick (10)	208
Christie Batty (10)	209
Lina Kumasaka (7)	209
Samir Gohil (9)	210
Liam Hobbs (8)	210
Leanne Anderson (10)	211
Charlotte Watson (8)	211
Oliver Herring (9)	212
Oliver Cooke (9)	212
Thalia Gorvin (10)	213
Elliot Street (7)	213
Harry Chevis (8)	214
Eleanor Rendell (8)	214
Beatrice Nugent (8)	215
Sebastian Wylie (8)	215
Emily Spurdell (8)	216
Josh Reynolds (9)	216
William Brittain (10)	217
James Warren (7)	217
Luke Witts (10)	218
Ryan Bunce (9)	218
Thomas Spackman (8)	219
Indya Grand (9)	219

Westlea Primary School, Swindon

Bethany Williams (10)	219
Gordon Wai (8)	220
Sophie Peart (8)	220
Tess Pringle (8)	220
Hannah Sharp (10)	221

Whitehall Primary School, Bristol

Elijah Begen (7)	221
Martha Hayes (8)	222
Chantelle-Rose Clarke	222
Chloe Nicholls (10)	223
Nathan Fuller (9)	223
Flora Begen (11)	224

The Poems

Swimming

Swimming is fun
swimming is cool
especially when I
jump in the pool.

In my life
my favourite thing,
is when Saturday comes
and I go swimming.

Myles Billinge-Jones (10)
Baydon St Nicholas CE Primary School, Marlborough

Pink's Pig

Pink had a pig
The pig was big
The pig ate lots
He had some spots
The pig grew fat
So lay on the mat
Pink's pig was ill
He'd had his fill.

Billy Bushnell (10)
Baydon St Nicholas CE Primary School, Marlborough

What Am I?

Blood sucker
Light hater
Night watcher
Night flyer.

What am I?
A bat..

George Hill (10)
Baydon St Nicholas CE Primary School, Marlborough

What Am I?

Mouse snatcher,
Good catcher,
Bird eater,
Big beater,
Bird glider,
Bad hider,
Big bird,
No word,
Big claws,
Bad snores,
Spotty coat,
Killed a goat,
White spots,
Hate dots.

What am I?
A buzzard.

Thomas Geary (10)
Baydon St Nicholas CE Primary School, Marlborough

What Am I?

Meat eater,
Rabbit beater,
Fast racer,
Cat chaser,
Big paws,
Sharp claws,
Likes to play,
Every day,
Sleeps at night
Growl it might
Wags its tail
Attacks the mail.

What am I?
A cute and cuddly dog.

Sophie Norman (11)
Baydon St Nicholas CE Primary School, Marlborough

Who Am I?

Bug squisher
Nose picker
Mud pie maker
Chocolate taker
Loud screamer
Day dreamer
Food thrower
Bottom shower
Girl hater
Bedtime later
Big hitter
Dropping litter.

Who am I?
Run for cover . . .
I am a baby brother!

Harriet Silvester (10)
Baydon St Nicholas CE Primary School, Marlborough

My Cat Bella

My cat Bella
Is blacker than black
She is a happy, fun-loving
Cuddly cat.

My cat Bella
Is madder than mad
She climbed up the chimney
Then jumped on my dad.

My cat Bella
Is blacker than black
Madder than mad
And
Slicker than slick!

Georgie Byfield (10)
Baydon St Nicholas CE Primary School, Marlborough

War

I can see the bombs showering to the ground like needles.
Men battle for their lives and their country.
Spitfires flying overhead in great packs.
People fire guns, charging at the enemy.
Tanks wiping out twenty people at a time.

I can hear the sound of gunfire all around,
People dying and bombs exploding.
Then I hear the sound of tanks trudging forward
And the planes flying overhead.

I can feel the squelching mud beneath my shoes,
My blisters getting bigger by the minute.
Rain pouring down my neck like a shower of nails.
The ground shakes as bombs explode.
I can feel the fear of all the men around me.
I can feel the silence of all the dead
And the hunger of the living.
I felt a bullet pierce my skin like a knife through hot butter.
The weight of my body dropped to the ground
And I felt the oozing mud pile into my wound.

Jordan Rosenberg (10)
Baydon St Nicholas CE Primary School, Marlborough

What Am I?

I can move as fast a cheetah
Or as slow as a snail.

I eat through rock
And cut through soil.

I can destroy buildings
Or produce power.

What am I?
Water!

Ryan Fourniss (11)
Baydon St Nicholas CE Primary School, Marlborough

War

I could hear men crying out before a brave death.
The buzzing of bullets narrowly missing me.
The tanks groaning while being sucked up by the mud.
The rat-tat-tat of gunfire, coming from enemy lines.

I could see brave soldiers defeated.
The enemy slouching through the mud.
Bombs exploding, ripping men apart.
Planes dodging gunfire, sometimes exploding.

I felt the sadness all around me.
A bullet ripping my ear apart.
The rain dripping over my neck like ice blocks.
The blisters under my feet exploding.

Philip Ball (11)
Baydon St Nicholas CE Primary School, Marlborough

Home

I see a sea of grass,
It rolls from horizon to horizon,
I look and think; I'm home.

I travel on and see my house,
I see the donkey,
I see the dog and I know I'm home.

I see my father and mother,
I see my brothers and sisters,
I look at them and I'm certain I'm home.

I am lucky,
Lots of my fellow knights didn't make it,
I go inside and I'm glad I'm home.

Emmie Rose Price-Goodfellow (11)
Baydon St Nicholas CE Primary School, Marlborough

Troublemakers' Guide

All you naughty children,
Listen to me well,
If you want to torment adults,
I'll teach you to make hell!

Put salt in their cups of tea,
Put grapes on their chairs,
Put mud on their hoovered floors,
Go on, it's a dare!

Never do your homework,
Never clean your room,
Never help with the cooking,
No sweeping with that broom!

Did you like my poem?
Did I give you some ideas?
I hope this little ditty,
Will reduce your mum to tears!

Holly Marriott Webb (11)
Baydon St Nicholas CE Primary School, Marlborough

Neverland

There was a man,
Who lived in Yorkshire,
He had no shirt,
Or underwear,
But then one day,
He went abroad,
To Neverland,
And to this day,
He's still there,
With no shirt,
Or underwear.

Toby Kacary (10)
Baydon St Nicholas CE Primary School, Marlborough

What Am I?

I can move as softly as the moonlight
Or as wildly as a demented chicken,
Occasionally I can destroy buildings
When I get angry,
I can cool things down or blow things away.

What am I?
The wind.

Malcolm Billinge-Jones (10)
Baydon St Nicholas CE Primary School, Marlborough

The Fat Frog

There was a big fat frog,
Who looked like a warthog.
He liked to play
In the hay
Until one day he got lost in the fog
And fell head first into a bog.

Rosemary Bird (11)
Baydon St Nicholas CE Primary School, Marlborough

The Reds Are Going To Turkey

The Reds are going to Turkey,
We're playing AC Milan
With the fans as our twelfth team member
We go all the way
And we'll be lifting the cup
At the end of the day.

Dominic Terrett (10)
Baydon St Nicholas CE Primary School, Marlborough

What Am I?

I have a long white neck with black beady eyes.
I have lovely white feathers and a bright orange beak.
I am proud but I like to nip and peck.
I swim gracefully on my clear blue lake.

What am I?

Rachel Nethercott (10)
Baydon St Nicholas CE Primary School, Marlborough

George

I know a man called George,
Who spends his life in a forge.
He works all day,
Doesn't have time to play
And never gets out of the gorge.

George Buck (10)
Baydon St Nicholas CE Primary School, Marlborough

Weeping Woman

Why is this woman weeping?
Perhaps somebody's died.
Broken glass with grief.
Perhaps her lover has left her.
Perhaps she is weeping
Because somebody wants to kill her.
Perhaps she's weeping
Because her newborn baby has died.
But the grief will end soon.

Sam Dixon (10)
Becket Primary School, Weston-super-Mare

Cat

Cats
Cloudy
Like a pillow
Sleek as an otter
Teeth, sharp
Looking for mice
Fleas
Itchily jump
Feathery
Tail swishes
Claws pointy
Like a witch's fingernail.
Cat's hairs
Sweet as a dream
Slinky
She crawls
On the floor.

Dannielle Francis (10)
Becket Primary School, Weston-super-Mare

Weeping Woman

Warm
Salty tears dripping from
Her face
And desperate eyes
Shining like the wheels on a bike.
The tears are crystal clear
Waiting to be wiped away
Her hat is like a colourful
Rainbow
Diamond-shaped hands
Silver as a lock with a round keyhole.

Shani Hedges (9)
Becket Primary School, Weston-super-Mare

Horse And Foals

Fresh
Frosty air
Effervescent

Tree bark
Rough as a
Bumpy road

River
Waving down
The stream

Wonderful
Swaying wind
Blowing around
The countryside

Vines
Drooping over
The swaying river

Dark
Gloomy sky
Waving around
The area.

Crispy
Crunchy sound
Of the leaves
Crunching on the floor.

Ashleigh Richards (9)
Becket Primary School, Weston-super-Mare

Horses

Grass
Clammy
Waterlogged,
Slimes and oozes.

Leaves
Rustling on trees
Wind is groaning
Like a moody person.

Countryside
Smells as aromatic
As a farm.

Fresh air
Transparent
As a glass ball.

Ground
Crunchy as
Frozen
Ice.

Amie Pickles (9)
Becket Primary School, Weston-super-Mare

Horses And Foals

Eyes crystal-black
Tail swings like a troubled thought
Ears soft leopard-skin
Sleek as a cheetah
Horses galloping, boomingly
Dark ground waterlogged
River pushing lonely rocks.

Nanine Balchin (9)
Becket Primary School, Weston-super-Mare

Cat

Cat biscuits
Crunchy, hard
Milk, cream, cold, fresh
Cat food sloppy, gooey, meaty.

Cat sleek
As a cheetah
Teeth as jagged
As a sleepless night.
When she cries
Her tears turn into diamonds
And skid like ice across her face.

In the garden
She waits to pounce on her enemy.
When she's outside
Her wild green eyes
Watch the birds fly by.

Amy Dillon (10)
Becket Primary School, Weston-super-Mare

Horse And Foal

Horse's tail furry as a cat.
Fresh grass scratches with sharp leaves,
Smelling of fruit cake,
Bumpy knees, rough as a playground floor.

Nose black like night,
Teeth crystal-white,
Eyes are like the sparkling sun,
Crumbly snow looks like their face.

Lips are greasy as a frying pan,
Mouth, yucky and slimy,
Eyebrows fluffy as a pillow,
Belly fat as a mushroom.

Kelly Hancock (10)
Becket Primary School, Weston-super-Mare

Horses And Foals

Mighty horses, strong like metal,
Tree sways like waves
Horses galloping while the foals stand silently
Smooth, silky
Brown like a new gate
White like a shocked face
I can taste cold, frosty air
While the horses stand speechlessly.

Melissa Cross (10)
Becket Primary School, Weston-super-Mare

Weeping Woman

Why is this woman weeping?
Perhaps her husband's left her.
Her melancholy is sharp and hurtful,
And empty as a desert.
Maybe sharp, shiny glass went in her
Like a broken friendship.
Maybe she is lost.

Michael Puddy (10)
Becket Primary School, Weston-super-Mare

Horses And Foals

Horses are powerful like speeding winds,
Horses neighing while the water is swaying,
Horses neighing in the wind,
White horse clean as the cleanest rubber,
Beautiful tree swaying in the wind,
Around horses I smell country air.

Amanda Pepper (9)
Becket Primary School, Weston-super-Mare

Ophelia

Peacefully floating in the speechlessly
Cold black water.
Ophelia's soul crying
Over her lost lover.
Her face is as white as a crystal chalk,
Her soul dies peacefully but painfully.
Her wretched troubles are over because
Her melancholic feelings are dead.

Alex Bloomfield (10) Joe Sandic & Connor Morss-Ford (9)
Becket Primary School, Weston-super-Mare

Smooth Cat

Cat, soft, smooth,
Looks extremely frightened,
Eyes like dark holes in the earth,
Smell of fish blended with sweet perfume,
Purring, rubbing ears, stretching lazily,
Whining, crystal tears fall onto face,
Happy, content, satisfied.

Jade Trevitt (10)
Becket Primary School, Weston-super-Mare

The Weeping Woman

Tears as heartbroken as a hurt child.
Did someone die?
Is she lost?
She is a-gloom with grief
And her face is as broken as binoculars.
Her life is an empty desert.

Toby Leigh & Declan Whittle (10)
Becket Primary School, Weston-super-Mare

Dark As A Midnight Dream

I looked up at the shimmering stars above
They were in the shape of a sparkling firework
It came alive
The world started spinning
Slower and slower as I walked further
Away from a shadow.
I thought it must be mine until I started to walk
It stayed there still as a stone.
Suddenly I heard a voice.
It whispered,
'I am your dream
That is why you can't see me
Only my shadow is to be seen.'
As I left my dream I saw all the stars again
This time they were in the shape of Guy Fawkes.

Kryzten Dellow (9)
Becket Primary School, Weston-super-Mare

Cat

Softly lying on the carpet.
Dark colours
Dark milky fur
Stripes.
Brown circle eyes looking around.
Whiskers.
Dusty lines
Like a cotton strip
Nose is like half a sparkling diamond.
Mouth
Damp tongue protruding.
Watching birds everywhere!

Hannah Hallworth (9)
Becket Primary School, Weston-super-Mare

Cat

Eyes
On the look-out
Wild green eyes
Watch birds in mist.
Sharpest
Claws teeth,
Pink velvet nose.

Teeth
White as an ill child.
Purring like a bus engine.
Cat
Cuddly cute
Softest fur about.

Gareth Gilpin (9)
Becket Primary School, Weston-super-Mare

Cat

Cat
Soft
Smooth
Eyes like
Dark holes
In the ground.
Cat smells like
Salmon fish
Mixed up with perfume.
He purrs and scratches ears,
Stretches out in front of a fire.
Happy,
Contented,
Satisfied.

Robert Perry (10)
Becket Primary School, Weston-super-Mare

The Sea

A beautiful thing,
Sparkling sea green.
Many tales have been
Woven round it.

It is the greatest prison,
Many creatures live in it
Thinking in silver mail.

No one knows
How deep it goes,
A mind beyond measure
Thought up its complexity.

It give us much pleasure,
But also gives us grief
When it seeks revenge
For our meddling
And destruction,
Of its beauty and grace.

Jack Langham (10)
Bishops Cannings CE Primary School, Devizes

What Am I?

I help people learn,
When you turn me on,

Especially with homework,
I am powered by a plug,

You can paint or play games,
If you break me,

You can replace me,
What am I?

Matthew Woods (11)
Bishops Cannings CE Primary School, Devizes

World War I

I can see bombs over my head
Squishy mud and mould below my feet
Planes falling in the distance
Men praying for their lives.

I can feel pain in my frozen boots
Men dropping dead beside me
Dampness soaking through the holes in my trousers
Warm blood streaming down my arm.

I can hear crashes and screaming around me
Wind blowing in my ears
The bangs from the guns
Then a shout, my shout, then darkness
I'm gone, I'm dead.

Elysia Walker (9)
Bishops Cannings CE Primary School, Devizes

The First World War

I can see the planes flying above me,
There are men falling dead to the floor
The noises of shotguns almost deafening me
The soggy, damp floor of the trench is horrible beneath my feet.

I feel terrified, I could die any second
My head is throbbing with the noise outside
My feet are frozen, I can hardly move them
I hear screaming people, they know death is coming
Suddenly . . .

Bang!
Bang!
Bang!

Amy Holt (8)
Bishops Cannings CE Primary School, Devizes

Save The Planet

Stackpole taught us to recycle rubbish,
Not drop it on the floor.

They also taught us to turn the light off
Before we go out the door.

We are very bad at saving water
Making sure the taps don't drip.
Of course we've learnt a lot from
This Stackpole trip.

Cleaning up beaches is very important
Otherwise animals may perish
Don't chuck things into the sea
We don't want to lose the creatures we cherish.

Serran Aziz (11)
Bishops Cannings CE Primary School, Devizes

Thunder And Lightning

Lash, crash, bash, the thunder goes,
The night is flooded with rain
Aerial poles are struck down
Cables snap, trees ignite
People run to hide
Rain hammers down on people
And the ground
TVs turn off because of the power cut
People are scared by the crashing of clouds
Lash, crash, bash,
Is the sound of thunder and lightning.

Jack Braine (11)
Bishops Cannings CE Primary School, Devizes

What Am I?

I can flap my wings as hard as can be,
But I don't like eating frozen peas,
I like seeds,
But I don't like sitting on weeds,
My wings are very long,
They are also very strong,
I have a long beak,
I also like to peek,
My eyes are very big,
And I like to dig.

Amber Linsley (11)
Bishops Cannings CE Primary School, Devizes

Silence

Silence is like a swan sailing silently down a drifting river.
Silence sounds quiet and lonely.
Silence tastes like hot chocolate running down your throat.
Silence reminds me of a newborn lamb.
Silence feels like a gentle breeze blowing on your arms.
Silence smells like sweet summer flowers.
Silence looks like a clear empty swimming pool.

Sophie Hay (8)
Bishops Cannings CE Primary School, Devizes

Fear

Fear is black like my dad's hair.
It smells like a rubbish bin.
It tastes like a shaking scull.
It sounds like a werewolf.
It looks like a ghost.
It reminds me of Doctor Who.

Laura Drew (7)
Bishops Cannings CE Primary School, Devizes

Love

Love is pink like a heart that's gone pale.
It smells like sweet strawberries.
Love tastes like strawberry rock that's just been made.
It feels like a beating heart.
Love sounds like someone's playing a violin.
It looks like a rose.
Love reminds me of my cat because my cat has soft fur.

Sarah Carroll (8)
Bishops Cannings CE Primary School, Devizes

What Am I?

I have a twitchy nose,
But I have no clothes!

I love to play
And I am very tame!

I run round in a ball
And I come when you call!

I live in a cage,
But I die of old age!

Charlotte Little (11)
Bishops Cannings CE Primary School, Devizes

Happiness

Happiness is yellow like a bright sun.
It smells like fresh apples.
It tastes of sweets.
Happiness feels like a pot of gold.
It sounds like wind.
Happiness looks like a fairy.

Rachel Holt (7)
Bishops Cannings CE Primary School, Devizes

Water

I can visit the world,
Or stay in one place,
I can be in a cool drink,
If you're running a race.

I can kill everyone
And they won't survive,
If I wasn't here,
You wouldn't be alive.

I can sink a boat,
When my waves are high,
All of the people,
Will probably die.

I can make a flood,
As high as you can see,
I'm always alive,
Wherever you see me.

You will always find me,
Wherever you travel,
I can make puddles,
In your gravel.

I can break your house,
In only one wave
And I can make,
A very big cave.

Oliver Hector (10)
Bishops Cannings CE Primary School, Devizes

Fire

The fire
Warms itself

It burns wood and paper
Then it turns into vapour.

Fire burns
Smoke everywhere, killing everything it touches

The colour, the flame
The more fierce the fire.

Fire spreads
Looking for things to burn.

Searching every place,
But leaving no trace.

Emily Wellbelove (11)
Bishops Cannings CE Primary School, Devizes

A Poem

Silent and slow,
I slowly grow,
I have a shell,
I'm always well,
I can never kill,
I never become ill,
I live on the ground,
But I'm not very round,
I'm not very tall,
But tiny and small.

Jordan Hicks (11)
Bishops Cannings CE Primary School, Devizes

A Spider Upon My Pillow

One night when I awoke,
I saw a tiny spider
Sat upon my pillow,

I saw him again and again.

The poor little thing,
Lost and lonely
Without his spider folk.

I told my friends,

They didn't believe me,
Especially when,
I said
That my little spider friend
Spoke!

He spoke of the future,
Of what was to come.

He took me to places
You could never imagine:

Frosty forests far away,
Dusty deserts clear as day.

Icy mountains way up high,
Riding on eagles in the sky.

Magical caves full of gold,
Deep-sea wonder ever so old . . .
And

To another world where
My spider found his friends
Said goodbye
And left.

Tansy Dando (11)
Bishops Cannings CE Primary School, Devizes

What Am I?

If you eat me you will get poisoned
You will not die,
But you will survive
I live outside, but sometimes I hide
What am I?

I travel very slow,
I have no toes.
I eat mud to make my home,
But I don't have a cone.
My body is long,
But not too long
What am I?

I cough up hair balls
I think it's very cool
My owners are old
Well that's what I'm told
I have a cute button nose
And my fur is very fluffy
What am I?

Ruby Francis (11)
Bishops Cannings CE Primary School, Devizes

The Peregrine Falcon

The peregrine falcon swooping by,
Faster than a cheetah
Faster than I.
With steady wind catching its wings,
How soft its wings are in the spring.
A strike of lightning hitting its prey
The speed, strength, beauty and the way
The way of this incredible weapon
Of this incredible creature
They way of an incredible *bird!*

Drew Kewley (11)
Bishops Cannings CE Primary School, Devizes

What Am I?

I am blazing hot
I can burn down a house
Things run away from me
Like a person or a mouse.

I can make water steam
I can melt ice cream
I can kill a million people
Burn them all alive
I can even warm up a nice apple pie

I am not very nice
I could light cigarettes which is bad
But when people die I do feel sad

But I do useful things
Like warm up a house
But I can still burn it down.

Jake Grover (11)
Bishops Cannings CE Primary School, Devizes

The Book

This book
Has been took,
The children are glad,
It wasn't sad.

The book was about a lion
Which got stuck in some iron,
It was quite magical
But the book was not tall.

Ah-ha it's been found
In a doggy pound,
The book was in a suitcase
It was wrapped in some lace.

George Dunford (11)
Bishops Cannings CE Primary School, Devizes

Storm

Bash! Crash! Lash!
Goes the thunder.

Rushing rain falls down hard on
My window like stones
Being thrown into the sea.

Whirling wind
Swirls around
My house
Like a whirlpool.

Animals take cover under trees as
People sleep like bees.

Thunder and lightning
Coming out of the sky like darts
Being thrown into the ground.

Rain is getting louder. *Bang! Bang!*
Thunder is getting louder. *Bash! Bash!*
Wind is getting fiercer. *Swoosh! Swoosh!*

Bang! Bash! Swoosh! Bang! Bash! Swoosh!

Lauren Hookings (11)
Bishops Cannings CE Primary School, Devizes

Grizzly Bear

I've seen a grizzly bear
With overflowing hair.

Some bears are tall
Whilst others are small.

The grizzly bear is strong
Strong enough to break a gong.

The grizzly bear could move a boulder
When it gets older.

Matthew Lever (11)
Bishops Cannings CE Primary School, Devizes

Trees

A number of times I have fallen
But yet I will grow again
It takes a while for me to recover
But I am always there.

I was planted twenty years ago
When times were not like this.
They wore bright clothes it was cool
They didn't dress like you at all.

Bethan Lightowler (10)
Bishops Cannings CE Primary School, Devizes

Hawk

I am a hawk
I have an ear-piercing screech
I can fly high
But I can fly low
I am the creature that brings fun to hunters,
They may have fun but I don't
After I've been hiding
It's a joy to hunt mice in the outside again.

Milan Johnson (10)
Bishops Cannings CE Primary School, Devizes

Anger

Anger is red
Like the Devil's horns.
Anger sounds like all the horrible sounds put together.
Anger tastes like petrol being poured all over your tongue.
Anger smells like burnt tobacco.
Anger feels like rough gravel.
Anger looks like a mean face glaring at you.

Michael Wall (9)
Bishops Cannings CE Primary School, Devizes

Sadness

Sadness is light blue,
Like a cloudless sky.
It tastes like apple pie without ice cream.
It looks like tears running down your face.
It reminds me of a heart breaking.
It sounds like someone is crying.
It feels like nobody is there.

Sarah Jane Hunt (8)
Bishops Cannings CE Primary School, Devizes

What Am I?

I am a predator,
I swoop down on my prey
In the dead of night.

I can travel very slow,
Or very fast.

I see my prey in the dark
And swoop down silently for the kill,
I am an owl.

Oliver Powlesland (11)
Bishops Cannings CE Primary School, Devizes

Happiness

Happiness is yellow like the hot sun in the morning.
It smells like daisies on the bright green grass.
It tastes like sweet sugar in a blue and white bowl.
It feels like a warm heart.
It sounds like jingle bells.
It looks like a sparkly rainbow.

Abbie Coleman (8)
Bishops Cannings CE Primary School, Devizes

Horses Haikus

Horses are great fun,
They are also great to ride,
They jump really high.

Some are really smart,
They are all different sizes
And some spook a lot.

They can go quite fast,
Some of them are very tall,
They are all so cute.

Hannah Weston (11)
Bishops Cannings CE Primary School, Devizes

Frogs

Frogs, frogs
Pouncing on their prey
Crawling all around
Eating every day.

Frogs, frogs
Pouncing into a stream
Trying to eat
Are they having a dream?

Frogs, frogs
Bouncing off a tree
Spitting poison
Thinking of me!

Adam Watson (9)
Forest & Sandridge CE Primary School, Melksham

The Carnival

Bang, clang, boom
The carnival's on its way
Clap, snap, yap
We're sure to enjoy the day
Crash, bash, smash
We can hear the band
Crash, bash, bang
It can be heard across the land
Swish, zoom, clash
Just listen to that beat
Twang, whang, vroom
Come and join me in the street.

Rhys Dunn (10)
Forest & Sandridge CE Primary School, Melksham

My Hedgehog

My hedgehog can curl
My hedgehog can crawl
My hedgehog can come out at night
My hedgehog can hide
My hedgehog can sleep
My hedgehog can have babies
My hedgehog can knock things down
My hedgehog can prick people.

Candice Walters (7)
Forest & Sandridge CE Primary School, Melksham

Ice Hockey Haiku

The skid of a skate,
The smack of a hockey stick,
Somebody's sent off.

Henry Meakin (10)
Forest & Sandridge CE Primary School, Melksham

My Lovely World

My world is lovely
There are big tall trees that blow around in the wind
All the rivers flow quietly under bridges
The grass goes side to side
There are lovely parks for children to play in
And in the town there are lots of shops
The pet shop is the best
You can see people walking in and out with their fluffy dogs.
All the lovely schools
When you drive past you can see people playing with friends.
We have families and houses
But sometimes boys and girls spray graffiti on walls
And bullies bully little ones or call people names
They also drop litter on the floor on purpose.
Why do people spoil the world, why?

Karis Simmons (8)
Forest & Sandridge CE Primary School, Melksham

Our World

The plants are growing very quickly
And it's getting near to spring.
The kittens and the lambs will be born soon
Also the beaming sun will come out.
The river will keep on flowing
And the trees will be swaying in the wind.
People will play in their swimming pools
And play in the park with friends.
All the lovely rainbows come out when it's nice
And all the animals will go out in the fields.
When everyone is cheering and laughing,
The day must have begun.

Samantha Purves (8)
Forest & Sandridge CE Primary School, Melksham

Our Lovely World

My world is a wonderful place,
The trees are full of fruit and blossom in the spring.
The flowers bloom every day
The animals gallop and play
There are wonderful rainbows
With wonderful colours of reds and blues and others
The rivers flow quietly under the bridge
The beaming sun rises in the morning and goes down at night
The birds sing a pretty and quiet song in the morning
Everybody has good friends that are loving and caring
The trees blow in the wind and give people shade
The children play and it is such a joy to see them
The wonderful schools help children to learn
All the wonderful statues make life interesting
We are very lucky because we have warm homes and food
But!
Some people ruin our wonderful life
They throw litter on the floor
They hurt people
They spray graffiti on walls
They steal
So people should stop doing all these things
Because our world is so lovely.

Hannah Webb (7)
Forest & Sandridge CE Primary School, Melksham

What Is Pink?

Pink is sometimes the sky,
Way, way, way up high,
Pink is for a happy feeling,
Pink is for love hearts
Pink is for your skin,
Pink comes in the rainbow,
My favourite colour is pink.

Laura Park (9)
Forest & Sandridge CE Primary School, Melksham

Our World

My world is a beautiful place with amazing trees that give us fruit
Lovely rivers and streams that flow quickly past me
The pretty pink flowers shoot up quickly in spring
Love is a wonderful thing that most people have
The sunrise and sunset are beaming in the sky
All the animals, all furry and cute, all the horses galloping
All the healthy food and drink
The children play and it is such joy
The birds sing and tweet in the shady tree
All the wonderful weather
All the pretty stars and planets like Mars
People can be very good friends, their friendship never ends
The wind that brushes through the trees
The sky is bright and clear
The pond has scaly, shiny fish and lily pads
The sun burns my skin as I have been standing here for ages
Our world is a beautiful place.

Rachel McNally (8)
Forest & Sandridge CE Primary School, Melksham

Our Perfect World

The lovely pink flowers and the fruit in the trees with berry bushes
Sunny pond with lovely lily pads and fish
The sunrise is coming with a clear sky and fantastic singing birds
Cows eating the grass and making a mooing sound and drinking
out of a trough
We have purple, yellow and orange flowers
Lovely leaves with white blossom from the tree above
Children playing in blossom and leaves and feeding the cows grass
We're looking at the orange fish in the pond
With lovely clear water and a swing by the side
To people it's a secret like a secret place.

Molly Adams (7)
Forest & Sandridge CE Primary School, Melksham

Lonely

I was lost on a beach
It was lonely
I had sand in my toes
I was scared
I was lost
I wanted an ice cream
I was scared to turn around
I was only five years old
I only had sand, people and sea
I did not know what to do
But, I found my family in the end.

Katie Gulliford (9)
Forest & Sandridge CE Primary School, Melksham

What Makes A Perfect World?

The beautiful sea full of fish and other sea creatures
The jungle full of animals
The sunlight, shining everywhere
People being loving and kind to other people
The trees giving us fruit
Nature appearing every spring
Families to love and pets to look after
Friends to play with and houses to play in
Fields to play in in the countryside and taking walks
Everyone loves our world.

Thomas Clover (8)
Forest & Sandridge CE Primary School, Melksham

Dolphin

Dolphin, dolphin, swimming very fast
Gliding through the ocean as little fish pass.
Dolphin, dolphin, jumping very high
Leaping from the water to see the birds fly.

Courtney Bridger (9)
Forest & Sandridge CE Primary School, Melksham

I Like . . .

I like coffee,
I like corn,
I like sandwiches,
I like prawns.

I like peas,
I like ham,
I like toffee,
I like jam.

Eleana Murphy (7)
Forest & Sandridge CE Primary School, Melksham

Fishing

Throwing some sharp sticks
Fishing, skimming the clear surface
Heaving on the oars.

The splashing of the fish
Reeds swishing in the warm breeze
Huge fish caught by men.

Sailing on a boat
Determined to catch some fish
Coming home for tea.

I am so hungry
Haven't caught a fish
There's a bite, *whoopee!*

Putting the sails up
On the massive River Nile
Cannot wait for tea!

Owen Burnell (8)
Headley Park Primary School, Bristol

Building The Pyramids

Building, working hard
Building the pyramids
Angry, upset, sad.

Hearing snakes hiss slowly
People talking with sadness
The winds of Egypt.

See sandstorms, *horror!*
Slaves are building the pyramids
Sand and people lost.

Egypt lost in sand
Horrible place to stay here
Gone forever, mad.

Feel mad, upset, sad
Don't pay for work for good
Angry we work here.

Hear Death's door, pain
People dying from building
Children must be safe.

Ashleigh Britton (9)
Headley Park Primary School, Bristol

Fishing

Shouting, splashing
Rod in the Nile
Waiting and waiting
A pull on the string
Determined to catch
Some slippery, sliding fish
Chop them up and put them
In a dish.

Amy Ward (9)
Headley Park Primary School, Bristol

Egypt

Death mask, mummies sleep
Arising from the dark deep
Even though they're dead.

Cooking on a fire
Hot fish on the boiling stove
Eating merrily.

Children are starving
Rushing, got to get it done
Heat is sizzling.

Cooking foreign food
Chilli and spices
Dig in kids, enjoy.

Dead mummies everywhere
Killing people every day
So scared - can't go back!

Henry Harper (9)
Headley Park Primary School, Bristol

Working In A Pyramid

In the pyramid
Helping out a little bit
The banging is quite loud.

Burying people
Tired out, can hardly breathe
Feeling very numb.

Feeling very scared
Piles of sand are everywhere
Death looks unpleasant.

Death mask; all gold
Pharaohs had lots of money
Feeling quite afraid.

Harry Browning (9)
Headley Park Primary School, Bristol

Building A Pyramid

Getting all sweaty
Inside a pyramid
Where traps spring up.

We are in Egypt
Building massive pyramids
With huge tombs.

Step on pyramid
Limestone bricks crash together
Sliding down the tombs.

Climbing up and down
Taking up limestone bricks
Going down again.

Heavy bricks fall down
People get worn out really quick
People sweating fast.

Jonathan Searle (9)
Headley Park Primary School, Bristol

Hunting For Food

Hunting through the forest
Nobody but me
Running through the atmosphere
Seeing trees swaying in the breeze
Seeing a snake
Chasing after it
Ha, ha
Caught it; some good food
Coming out of Egypt
Nobody but me
Now this is the end
For you and me.

Liam Norris (8)
Headley Park Primary School, Bristol

Hunting For Animals

We're searching for cows to eat
We're hunting to help grow food.

We are chasing animals to keep and then kill
We do this for a living for ever
But we will die because of our age.

We use slings to catch animals
To keep us humans alive and healthy.

We're setting our aim so we can get cow or goat to eat
Crawling on the ground so we can get food.

Shooting rocks and stones to try and catch animals
We are the humans who kill the animals
So we can live
To keep the human race alive forever.

Jake Burston (9)
Headley Park Primary School, Bristol

The Pyramid

I can see:
I can see the people as small as can be,
Staring and taking pictures of me
They are like tiny ants, so small they are like a blur
That's how small they are.

I can hear:
Squeaking mice
I can hear the pharaoh shouting at his slaves
I can hear everything
I can hear the queen as loud as thunder
I can hear the pharaoh like a powerful bull.

I can feel:
I can feel the wind crashing against me, like the heavy waves.

Josie Cameron (8)
Headley Park Primary School, Bristol

The Pyramids

What can you see?
I see tiny people like ants and pharaohs too
I see people talking to each other
The people are as small as mice
I see slaves milking a cow.

What can you hear?
I hear people building pyramids, *boom, boom!*
I hear people talking, like the bossy pharaoh
I hear people laughing as loud as a drill
I hear a bird crying like rain dripping; I think it broke its wing.

What can you feel?
I feel people building me up like I just don't care
I feel the hot sun beaming down on me like I'm its shield
I feel they have left me in the middle of nowhere
Now, I feel sweat dripping as slow as a snail.

Molly Quantick (8)
Headley Park Primary School, Bristol

My Egyptian Poem

I look around and I can see gold,
Beautiful gold glimmering like the yellow sun.
I take off my crown, I think it looks like cellophane on the sunset.
I see my slaves working hard as if they were robots
Doing whatever I say.

I hear babies crying as if they were lions roaring,
I hear slaves walking up and down
As if they were an escalator going up and down.

I can feel the fur on my throne as if it were leopard's skin
I can feel the wind blowing my hair as if it was an earthquake . . .
I am a goddess.

Georgia Elson (7)
Headley Park Primary School, Bristol

Poems About Egypt

Tugging on our nets
Waiting for a fish to catch
Searching all day long.

People shouting loud
Killing fish for their supper
Taking out their bones.

People washing clothes
Fish skimming along the Nile
Fishermen are skilled.

Feeling confident
Knowing I will catch a fish
Pleased I caught a fish.

Shouting out with joy
Because I caught a clownfish
Making the boat shake.

Fish are everywhere
Loads of them are being caught
They are people's lunches.

Matthew Hawkins (9)
Headley Park Primary School, Bristol

Pyramid

Blistering,
Boiling,
Hard at work
Slamming bricks
Making a noise
People sweat
A hard day at work
Finished, pyramid ready for
Tutankhamen.

Abigail Pratten (9)
Headley Park Primary School, Bristol

Sailing Up The Sleepy Nile

Fish
Alligators
Shimmering sea.
Rocks bashing
Paddles
Hoisting sails
Tired.
Hot
Determined
Water rushing.
Fish swimming
Out
Into
The
Mediterranean
Sea
Waves
Crashing
Into
The
Sea.

Charlotte Williams (9)
Headley Park Primary School, Bristol

My Egyptian Poem

I can see the sand
It is as hot and as bright as the sun
I can see birds flapping their wings
I can see the River Nile swishing
I can hear butterfly wings as soft as air
Birds eating prey
Horses running across the sand as fast as a race car
I can feel sand in my eye like burning hot coal
I feel like a tractor is running over me
I am a pyramid.

Jesse Payne (8)
Headley Park Primary School, Bristol

Sailing Up The Nile

Sitting in the boat
Most satisfied in the sea
I can see big fish.

Sailing in the lake
Hunting for fish in the sea
On a scorching day.

I can see bubbles
I'm staring at the fish breathing
You can hear people.

I can catch fish
I can hear people fishing
People are shouting.

Can I catch a fish?
People are catching fish
Yes, I caught a fish!

Megan Pope (9)
Headley Park Primary School, Bristol

Building The Pyramids

The sand was blowing
I saw hard men working to the day's end
I heard the men banging
I heard other men shout
We felt tired and worn out from the hard work
We are shouting like the sun rising in the breeze
They are shouting, lugging bricks
Carving the bricks
The men are saying, 'Heave-ho!'

Kimberley Sargent (9)
Headley Park Primary School, Bristol

Hunting For Food

In a hot desert
Casting a net in the lake
Then I feel so brave.

Throwing spears at trout
Hunting for food, see some meat
Flowers, sand, mud and trees.

In a scorching world
The Nile is cold and muddy
Hunting for food now.

I can catch a fish
I can trap an elephant
I can't grab a cat.

I can spot people
Sandy plains around me now
The island is huge.

Jessie Carey (8)
Headley Park Primary School, Bristol

My Egyptian Poem

What can you see?
I can see tiny people on horses, running
The horses are black and white like cows.

What can you hear?
I can hear workmen cutting wood to make boats
The workmen walked by like a ship sailing past.

What can you feel?
I can feel the ground shaking
It's the workmen digging a hole in the ground
I can feel the sun shining like a big light.

George Hancock (7)
Headley Park Primary School, Bristol

My Egyptian Poem

What can you see?
I can see a pharaoh and people that look like microscopic ants
What can you see?
I can see birds flying very high
What can you see?
I can see other pyramids.
            I am a pyramid.

What can you hear?
I can hear people shouting, they sound like snakes rattling in the grass
What can you hear?
I can hear birds singing
What can you hear?
I can hear raindrops coming.
            I am a pharaoh.

What can you feel?
I can feel the breeze
What can you feel?
I can feel the raindrops on me
What can you feel?
I can feel gold inside me.
            I am a pyramid.

Wesley Lewis Williams (8)
Headley Park Primary School, Bristol

My Egyptian Poem

I can see my glitter winking at me as if it were my slave.
I also see my husband Tutankhamen sitting on his gold and
                                    blue throne.

I can hear slaves asking me if I would like a drink
Like a lot of robots, people praying like nodding dogs.

I can feel the gold under my hands
And a stained royal blue cushion under my bottom and feet
My husband's hand over mine.
I am a goddess.

Jennifer Taylor (8)
Headley Park Primary School, Bristol

Dear Dad

Dear Dad,
While you were out . . .
The dog got in the car and drove it into a wall,
The cat made a hole in the roof,
(I really don't know how).
The huge cupboard with all the china fell over on purpose,
All the vases broke when I was outside.
A crack appeared in the middle of the table.
Half of the windows got smashed
When the dog saw a cat outside.
I was cleaning the house, honest
And the vacuum cleaner fell down the stairs
(And completely smashed).
All of your fresh tomatoes and other vegetables and fruits,
Oh and the flowers are completely destroyed.
The house is a *little* messy,
Other than that, everything is fine.

From your responsible daughter.

Harriet Seymour (9)
Horrington Primary School, Wells

Aliens

Aliens have come from outer space
With four green eyes, body covered with spots
They came from a planet which wreaks and rots
They came in a spaceship
Then quite amazingly
Asked me out for a cup of tea
They said in their gurgly voice
That they came from the planet Zog
Which looks like a dirty, smelly, old bog
They wanted to know what life was like
I told them, they gave me an alien bike
Aliens are quite nice you know
Sadly no one here will ever know.

Angus Morrice (9)
Horrington Primary School, Wells

My Favourite Pet - Jax

He flies through trees
As silent as night
If he sees prey
He soon takes flight.

He comes to the fist
If I give him a squawk
His name is Jax
Oh that Harris hawk!

He comes in the house
He raids the bin
Stale pizza's
His favourite thing.

He gets a banana
In his beak
He shakes his head
And covers our feet.

Jax, my favourite pet.

George Hill (8)
Horrington Primary School, Wells

A Most Unusual Toad

In the park a toad was walking
A heron flew down and started stalking
The toad saw a pond and began to jump
The heron waved his wand with a crash and a clunk
A flash and a bang!
The unusual toad turned into a man!
What happens next you'll have to wait and see
Does the man go away or does he stay for tea?

Emma Keene (7)
Horrington Primary School, Wells

Aliens Stole My Nightdress

In the middle of the night
Something gave me an awful fright.
I was lying in bed,
When I heard a voice, it said,
'I think this would suit you well,
Much better than that golden bell.'
It was then I looked outside my door
And do you know what it was I saw.
Two aliens with my nightdress,
They had left the house in a big mess.
I didn't really mind that much,
It would have just gone to another planet or such.
But next time,
Don't take mine.

Grace James (9)
Horrington Primary School, Wells

The Blue Horse

Shadows walk along the street,
I can hear clip-clop as a beat.
It is fast,
Like a blast
Flames come out of my window,
O, it was just a mane, not a flame.
There it was, the Blue Horse
Pushing on my gate with force.
Standing on its toes,
Pushing with its nose.
The cockerel crows
Shocks all.
The Blue Horse gone!
Tonight maybe I will see her again.

Ellie Massey (7)
Horrington Primary School, Wells

Lunch, Lunch

Lunch, lunch, I love lunch
The yoghurt called the Munch Bunch
Sausage rolls
Cheese with holes
And ice cream that is freezing cold
Wobbly jelly in my belly
I hate it if it is quite smelly
Everybody gather round
Look at all the food that's been found!

Jamie Tweed (8)
Horrington Primary School, Wells

The School Playground

In the school playground
children run around
up the corridor
and down around town
some are noisy
some are sound
in the school playground
children shout out
loud!

Freyja Chitty
Horrington Primary School, Wells

Toe Gnasher Kennings

Fish catcher
Night stalker
Toe gnasher
Day sleeper
Mouse chaser
Claw scraper
That's my naughty cat!

Isaac Stone (8)
Horrington Primary School, Wells

A Frankenstein

A Frankenstein
In the night?
That must have been
An awful fright!

A Frankenstein
In the house?
Even worse than a
Dirty, black mouse!

A Frankenstein
In the town?
Oh golly, oh gosh
Trying to steal the mayor's crown!

Who's got a Frankenstein costume?
I know . . .
Harry!

Nancy Lunnon (8)
Horrington Primary School, Wells

I Am Dreaming Of . . .

I am dreaming of . . .
a spacecraft on Mars!
I am dreaming of . . .
shiny new cars!
I am dreaming of . . .
lots of treats!
I am dreaming of . . .
loads of sweets!

I wake up . . .
and my room is empty!

Hayley Withers (9)
Horrington Primary School, Wells

The Old Oak Tree

As we've lived in our house
we've loved and loved the old oak tree.

Never, never, would we harm the old oak tree
The old oak tree gives shade to Max and me
And when Olsaan grows up under the tree will be three.
On summer days we climb onto a branch and eat our tea
On winter days we go out and chase away the fleas
Never, never would we want to see
The old oak tree go
And it hasn't, what glee!

Josh Cook (8)
Horrington Primary School, Wells

Sun And Moon

When the bright sun is out in the day
It shines warmly on you
And when the sun goes away
The bright shining moon comes out to stay.
Badgers and foxes and bats come to play
Millions of flashing lights
And the fairies come to sprinkle some magic
And then it is done.

Ellie Oliva-Knight (8)
Horrington Primary School, Wells

My Teacher

My teacher's imagination can run wild
      But mine is certainly more mild
She runs around like a loony
      Her name is Mrs Alicia Cloony
She loves midnight feasts, but hates big fat beasts
      She thinks she's so cool when she jumps right in her very own pool
That's Mrs Alicia Cloony.

Rosie Davies (8)
Horrington Primary School, Wells

The Fierce Cockerel And The Fox

'It was last night,' our teacher said,
'My neighbour was thinking of going to bed.
When he heard a load of squawks and bleats,
He went out to see what was distressing the fleets
And when he went out, oh what a sight
Something quite gruesome in the night.
A fox so very creepy and sly
(Well, for tasty chickens it was worth a try!)
The fox had got inside the chickens' coop
The chickens were so scared they started to poop!
There were goldy-brown feathers all over the floor
And there was a great big hole in the wire mesh door
The fox had got the cockerel by the neck
But the cockerel was tough and he started to peck
And kick at the fox's red furry tummy
It must have looked rather funny!
And then the fox slipped back into its hole
As he heard the chiming morning bells toll.
My neighbour stood and scratched his head
Then he said, 'My goodness I should be in bed!'

Anna Williams (9)
Horrington Primary School, Wells

My Best Friend

My dog is my best friend
I'm always the first she defends

She is always with me being so sweet
But is always looking for something to eat

She loves to play with her ball
But always comes when I call

We like to go for long walks
'Woof, woof,' and she always like to talk

She is big and black and Tessa is her name
She gives me big wet licks, but I love her all the same.

Danielle Hill (8)
Horrington Primary School, Wells

Sister Babysitter

Mum and Dad are going out
'Oh no!' I shout.
'Don't worry your sister's here.'
'That's worse,' I said with fear.
'We will be fine
I'll read you a book
And put you to bed.'
She said with a halo round her head.
Mum and Dad turn around
Horns grow on my sister's head
We go inside then she says,
'Put the kettle on
Read a book
Clean your teeth
And go to bed
Goodnight.'

Luke Jenkins (9)
Horrington Primary School, Wells

The River

Brown, murky water passing by,
Deep and cold, reflecting the colourful sky.
Gentle winds whistling past,
Cheeping birds flying fast.
Green trees swaying in the breeze,
Until the wind began to freeze.
Golden reeds just waiting there,
Watching the light grey hare.
Tiny ripples coming in,
Looking like an old man's skin.
Gentle river calming down,
As it flows through the delightful town.
We left the river when it went cold,
But there's still many secrets the river holds.

Gregory Chapman (11)
Kingsmoor Primary School, Bridgwater

The River Poem

Flowing down riverbanks gently
Carrying leaves fallen from trees.

Ripples are made by dancing fish
Making a dancing wish
In the underworld of water.

When the ripples crash and combined
They make a magical chime.
Ripples make sparkles full of diamonds,
Rubies, sapphires and emeralds.

Colours are mixed into a pot
Brown, green, grey and yellow
Fluttering about.

Once the ripples fade all
You can see is a mirror
Reflection of what's above.

The river goes on and on
Sometimes curving
Sometimes straight
It just keeps swaying
Past everything.
People sometimes fish for
Colourful fish swishing and
Swaying in open waters.
People sometimes have a picnic by
The river on a summer's day.
People sometimes hear cheeping of birds
Up in trees on people's luxury walks.

The river is a wonderful and magical place.

Ross Bowden (11)
Kingsmoor Primary School, Bridgwater

The River

The river is a person
Always changing, always full of life.

Bouncy ripples bound up the riverbank,
Tickling the elegant lilies standing tall and proud.

A shiny mirror reflects the river's surroundings,
Showing the world its colours.

Gentle sounds of small ripples soothe your mind,
Crashing and splashing all day long.

Lurking shadows protect the river's secrets.

Different colours of the river shine out like paint pots
Browns, greens and blues.

The surface of the river is like untouched silk
Smooth, shiny and soft.

Wavy ripples are perfectly formed
Smudging the artist's paintwork.

The ripples kick and punch the river on
Moving to a different place.

Ripples are wrinkles on an old man's hand
Swishing through the water.

Peaceful is the river
You could hear a silent whisper.

The river so silent, so beautiful!

Phoebe Fisher (11)
Kingsmoor Primary School, Bridgwater

River Poem

The water was so sparkly it was
like a priceless jewel.
The water was like a swish of a silk
sari on a summer's night.
Water was like an old, dull tortoise with
a rough patchwork shell.

Smooth, opalescent water was like a
chameleon changing colour to its background.
River was magnificently, extremely languid it
was like an army of slugs advancing slowly.
The calm, gentle water was as precious as
a gold, expensive ring.

River was like a collage on water as the
lilies and bushes reflected into the river.
River was dancing, the extremely, extraordinary
ripples were dancing fantastically.
Calm, gentle wind was gently blowing the
lilies from side to side.

Entertaining, elegant, extraordinary river was dancing
until it could dance no more.
Soothing, soundless water was so peacefully quiet
in the midday sun.
Jumping water was so slow you could not see
it moving.

Jonathan Hill (11)
Kingsmoor Primary School, Bridgwater

The River

Slow and sluggish,
small and precious,
still and silent.
The shiny river gleams,
showing dancing rays of light.
Then moving like a car,
quick in places, slow in others.

The river carries the leaf soldiers who
march in the breeze,
making ripples at their feet as they
stamp at ease.
In straight rows,
long rows,
thick rows,
short rows.
They never stop.
Slowly marching,
going through small holes until
the wind stops.
All scattered about.
Then they settle and rest,
until the next day when they gather again.

Ben Judge (11)
Kingsmoor Primary School, Bridgwater

River Poem

The river is an active crocodile escaped
From his cage.
It is a shiny red ruby.
It leaps on past anything in sight giving
A silent whisper.
Every splash you hear is the small, little fish
Making bubbles like a big bubble bath.
The smooth, relaxing river glanced in the
Scorching, hot, boiling sun.
On the green grassy banks the bushes
Sway in the gentle breeze wind.
It is like the bushes are the ends of a toothbrush
As they are so rough.
A swish of a silk sari is the sway
Of the calm river.
It sits on its surface slowly going
Along it feels as if the surface is touching
A barn owl's fluffy, furry, smooth fur.
The big, clear reflection is like
Someone's face in a shiny mirror.
It kicks and leaps down the river
Like a big, spotty cheetah swaying from
Side to side till it reaches
The end.

Sam Biddulph (10)
Kingsmoor Primary School, Bridgwater

The River

Soft and shiny,
Dark and black
The river is a silent cat.
A beautiful painting
Or a large balloon,
Deflating.

Surrounded by darkness
The dirty river is
For a while.
Its sluggish movements
Last a mile.

Swaying in the wind
Tall, thin reeds,
The river's many weeds.

'Ripples on the river,'
Soldiers commanded,
By the rain.
The river is their battle plain.

Nathan Creedy (11)
Kingsmoor Primary School, Bridgwater

Wind River

The bank the river tickled,
With arms long and watery,
An elegant dance,
Does the river's waves
With birds' placid tweeting.

River is a golden flower,
Petals fall
Into dazzled water,
Glittering, glittering,
Churning up light,
Like a great jewel box.

Child calm.
Boy bouncy.
Girl a graceful galloping horse.
Kicking, kicking, kicking,
Horses galloping on waves watery.

Insects a-spiralling, frogs a-creeping,
Across rocks, painted with gold.
Is the wind. Is the wind.

Sarah Parsons (11)
Kingsmoor Primary School, Bridgwater

My River

My river is like a magnificent oil painting
Made by Van Gogh,
I imagine a hidden underwater kingdom
The water is like a ballerina dancing
Till the end,
Graceful and glistening is a river's atmosphere,
It will make you relaxed and calm.

No more wind,
The river's died,
Because the wind has stopped,
It moans for more,
Reflection like sky, but it's Heaven,
The sound of the river is a gentle, trickling music,
It is like a dream,
That is my river
And my dream river only!

Gabriella Robinson (11)
Kingsmoor Primary School, Bridgwater

The River

The beautiful, light, graceful river,
Moves slowly as the wind takes it along,
Limping over lily pads,
Tickling fragile flowers,
The river is never to be still.

Silent! Silent!
Its noise is not there,
In quietness you can hear the birds
Singing their sweetest songs,
Shimmering sunlight reflects from the river.

As the gentle wind shivers the water
Into wrinkling ripples.
Calmly, the young river runs.

Emily Clyne (11)
Kingsmoor Primary School, Bridgwater

The River

The river is like a newborn child,
Incredible sunlight controlling the world,
A present you really wanted,
Quiet children working hard,
Queen's precious crown.

A horse trying to get there first,
Mirror reflecting every detail,
Like velvet to touch,
As blue as the sky,
Drink being poured into a cup.

Traffic you hear,
Trees swaying too,
Children bouncing on a trampoline,
Light catches ripples when bright,
Surface looks like ice.

Makes you feel happy,
Water dies when wind stops,
Glistens like a pool full of diamonds,
Wrinkly like an old man's hand,
Very peaceful.

Calming sound of water,
Lily pads stay still,
Further down you look, reflections are clearer,
Swiftly moving along,
Is the slow moving, noticeable river.

Victoria Elizabeth Chapman (11)
Kingsmoor Primary School, Bridgwater

The River

Skilled sun finished painting the river,
The wind smudges the perfect picture.
Delicate blues become pale whites
Calmness becomes slight urgency.
Until the wind fades
The sun repaints the precious painting.

Unknown secrets,
Covered by lurking shadows,
Choppy ripples protect and guard secrets.

Vibrant ripples,
Lolloping ripples,
Dancing ripples,
Soundless ripples,
Revealing ripples,
A graceful, enchanting dance.

A swish of smooth, untouched silk
That slowly flows.
Majestic, elegant, mysterious river.

Ffion Jones (11)
Kingsmoor Primary School, Bridgwater

The River

The water is kicking droplets one by one,
Pulling wildlife down the river,
Controlling the entire world.
Moving in its own magnificent way.
It is unrevealing, showing nothing.
It is a snakeskin pattern, old and used.
Beautifully showing the colours of the rainbow,
Beautiful and easy to admire.
It's the queen's long, wrinkly dress
It's like the velvet dress would shatter into a million pieces.
The dress is soothing, only letting out gentle, soothing sounds.
It was perfect in every way,
Flowing peacefully are old wrinkles,
Old wrinkles on an old man's hand.
Flowing are untamed ripples,
Like untamed animals in the wild.
It is happy and harmless,
Just very beautiful and perfect.
It was perfect and light,
As if God could lift it up in His hand.

Sophie Thyer (11)
Kingsmoor Primary School, Bridgwater

The River

Swaying reeds are guards,
Protecting the river's secrets,
Slow, smooth and gentle,
Is the tranquil river,
Ripples are wrinkles of an old man's hand,
Caused by the blow of the summer's breeze,
Young is river,
Always changing shapes,
Smooth, flat and untouched is the silky river,
Valuable, sparkling, priceless jewels,
Is the precious river,
Softly, majestically,
Flows the river calmly,
A swish of paint from the sun,
Fills the river's blank canvas,
Soft, smooth and cool,
Slippery is the feel,
Beautiful birds singing,
Soothe the mind magically,
A peaceful atmosphere,
Causes all problems to disappear . . .

Emily Easman (11)
Kingsmoor Primary School, Bridgwater

The River

River, as calm as paper,
Fluttering in the breeze.
Lots of mirrors making colours,
Making a rainbow river.
Flexible is a river when the river
Snake comes.
Angels create the heavenly river.

Fluffy clouds, calm blue sky,
Lush green trees all sink into the river.
Up the valley water splits,
Spacing from the current.

Jagged go the ripples
When nature breathes.
Dancing are the weeds,
While the breath is full.
Fish relax by the currents.

This is my river's view,
And only *my* river's view.
Nobody has the same view.

Nicholas Hughes (10)
Kingsmoor Primary School, Bridgwater

The River

The river is peaceful, calm and quiet,
Not a twitch or sound from the river,
River peaceful, calm and tamed,
The river so peaceful that all you can hear is the noise of birds,
The river soundless, quiet and calm,
The river noticeable and so delightful.

The elegant river flows down its pathway reflecting everything,
A chest of rubies, gold and diamonds glisten like the river,
The river reflects the sun's almighty power.

The river flowing by,
Reflecting the sun high in the sky,
Gentle winds blowing past,
The cheeping of birds going fast,
Ripples dancing, reeds swaying,
Moving in every direction.

Gentle winds follow the river,
As if it's the commander.

Nathan Bale (11)
Kingsmoor Primary School, Bridgwater

River

The calm river drifts forward
Brushing up any loose bits soundlessly.
All the sound is dead,
No noise at all.
On the murky dark river
Is the reflection of the beautiful surroundings.
Green trees, green bushes and a sparkling blue sky
Surrounds the precious river, it's like the most valued thing in the world
Ripples are wrinkles on an old man's hand.
Ripples are like grand steps,
Which would lead up to a rich mansion.
More ripples from fish
Making a mini whirlpool.
Before all of this,
A diving, magnificent fish makes a plop.
Birds hover over,
Hooting, cheeping and singing
Landing on the green trees
This river is extremely calm as it just drifts smoothly.

Robert House (11)
Kingsmoor Primary School, Bridgwater

River Poem

Soft wind awakes the water,
Sending ripples down the river,
Leaving a snake's skin on its tail,
Quickly and quietly blows the wind,
Then disappearing.

The soft, flowing gentle waters move elegantly.
Glistening in the sunlight is the river.
Generously gentle is the relaxing, calm river,
Mirroring its surroundings, dancing delicately.
The river lanquidly flows.

Delicate and untouched in calmness,
Water is gentle, disturbed by wind.
Debris travels with water,
Long distances are travelled.

The water feels like cotton and velvet,
Smoothing the weeds which live underneath.
River covers lots of land.
Creatures quietly move,
Whispering gently in the wind.
The beautiful countryside at its best.

Jack Plummer (10)
Kingsmoor Primary School, Bridgwater

The River

The river is amazingly adventurous,
Like Superman's best friend.
The river is extremely wide,
Looks like it has no end.
It is bumpy like an uprooted road,
Hopping on the lily pads is a green and slimy toad.

Calm like a motionless moon,
As delicate as a soggy tissue.
It gives a perfect reflection, just like a mirror,
The clouds' reflections are floating along,
Like some white snow on the surface.

The birds want fish for their tea.
Its ripples are an army,
Told its every move.
Birds are singing softly amongst the water's rushing.

It's cold like ice,
As dark as hot chocolate,
As calm as a tamed horse.
River persuades me to have a rest,
But rivers to me are really the best.

Scott Chidgey (9)
Kingsmoor Primary School, Bridgwater

The River

Ripples racing round the rocks,
Sneaking through the valley.
Deep dancing fish
Floating down the river.
Totally harmless flowing river
Is like a plate of liver.
Water flowing down the river
Looking like it's made of stone.

Snake-slithering water
Sneaking through the valley.
Quiet, quickly moving river
In-between the rocks.
The silent river is like everyone
With their mouths tied together.
The icy-cold river
Flowing down the valley.

When the river floated down the valley
It was calm.
As the river floated down the valley,
It looked extremely beautiful.
Exciting fish jumping in the river
Made it really fun.
The precious water was calmly
Floating down the river.

Michael Watts (10)
Kingsmoor Primary School, Bridgwater

The River Poem

River as calm as a sheet of glass,
Dancing with the wind,
Blue sky, green trees, reflecting on the river,
Swinging and swaying in the wind,
Blowing as a tornado pushing away,
Soothing wind gently passing by,
Fish are jumping out of the water making ripples,
As warm as a heatwave beaming down,
Magnificent animal, dodging everything,
River as fast as a speedboat,
Dodging every obstacle,
Underneath the surface is a dark river,
A fantastic river pushing anything,
The gentle river current scuttling by,
Taking anything with it.
Ripples as wrinkly as an old man,
River is so peaceful,
Birds flapping their wings and cheeping away,
Incredible wind forcing the river to move,
Top of the river all glossy and new,
Reflecting in the sun.

Bradley Quint (10)
Kingsmoor Primary School, Bridgwater

The River

The river, so soothing and beautiful,
A delicate butterfly,
Drifting past
A magnificent mirror,
A precious painting,
Glistening in the light.
Rays of radiant colours,
Beaming down from the sun.
A precious pearl,
A dazzling diamond,
A royal, red ruby,
A sparkling sapphire.
A smell of sweet dew,
A touch of velvety water.
Prancing proud like peacocks,
Like joyful, elegant, gliding swans,
Birds sing at this glorious sight.
The sloth-like river obeys the wind.
The wind is God.

Marie Gibbs (10)
Kingsmoor Primary School, Bridgwater

The River

Tortoiseshell, bright and green,
Gives a reflection like the river stream,
Soggy, slimy, soaking wet,
Tastes horribly of muddy saltwater,
Soothing, icy, calm, cold water,
Rushing everywhere amongst the ripples,
Runny honey and extremely soft,
Like some velvet in a loft,
Racing ripples rushing through the trees,
Gently the wind blows at the marvellous river,
Birds sing across the water,
Watching their reflections in the morning,
Royal river carries ripples,
Just like the postman carries post,
Quiet, noiseless, peaceful atmosphere,
All around the muddy bank,
Brass band amazing,
The cool river is too,
Harmless, silent, helps me think,
That's the river's special thing.

Christopher McMinn (10)
Kingsmoor Primary School, Bridgwater

The River

Calm, smooth, sky-blue, deep river,
One of the best I've seen.
Like a magnificent oil painting by Van Gogh
Graceful, glistening, gliding, gentle.
Dazzling water swaying in the breeze
Like wrinkles of an old man's hand.
I imagine a hidden underwater world
Beneath the dark sky-blue river.
Brightly coloured water, as young as a newly born baby
Such an incredible sight!

Water lolloping towards me
Kicking everything out of the way.
Cheeping birds make the river calm, sweet,
More opaque when you look through it.
The river is extremely noticeable
As noticeable as a queen's car.
It gives me safe, emotional feelings
Trickling down my spine,
Such an incredible sight!

Dancing river, peaceful and calm,
Sparkling fish make curled-shaped rings
Like fish gills opening for the fish to breathe.
Grassy, green, sky-blue reflections I see
With the leaves floating on top.
Such an incredible sight!

Lucy Kate Williams (10)
Kingsmoor Primary School, Bridgwater

The River

Never still is the river
Swerving, curling
Dancing in the wind.
Splashes of green, grey and yellow
Blend when the ripples charge.
But when the ripples die
A mirror is unfolded.

The water is a dancer
Twirling and whirling around many rocks.
Calm, majestic, is the river
Running repeatedly downstream.
But when it hits the sea
It turns rough and playful
Like the many white horses that live there.

Up in the high mountains
Where the river was created,
The love and care,
The planning,
The working
That God had completed.
So now we see this river
Now we give many thanks to God.

Stephanie Nicole Elkins (11)
Kingsmoor Primary School, Bridgwater

The River

A river is a precious pearl
Like a turtle shell,
As rough and jagged
As a waterfall.

Fish dancing in the sunlight,
Like birds chirping in the trees.
A rushing river's a pouncing cheetah cub,
Bouncing from rock to rock
Piercing, blinding light
Bouncing off the water like quick flying sparks.

An entertaining elephant
Crashes through the rocks,
As wrinkly as an old man's hand,
Are the ripples of the river.

Timothy Walker (10)
Kingsmoor Primary School, Bridgwater

Our Playground

Our playground
It's unique and entertaining.
Noisy, unpredictable and sociable.
As exciting and joyful as your birthday.
As crowded as Christmas shopping.
I feel as safe as a tree anchored by its roots.
Our playground.
A chance to do what we want!
But sometimes . . .
Our playground
Is dull and dismal
Miserable, gloomy and depressive.
As boring as going shopping for clothes with your mum
As lonely as being in space.
I feel vulnerable and insecure, as interested as watching paint dry.
Our playground.
The worst of all!

Bertie Adam, Leanna Bond (11) & Rosie Jenord (10)
Kingston St Mary CE Primary School, Taunton

The Magic Box

(Based on 'Magic Box' by Kit Wright)

I will put in the box …
The sound of the sea crashing against the shore,
The mane of a horse blowing in the wind
A tiger claw scratching a tree.

I will put in the box …
The wrinkles from an elephant's skin,
The sound of a lion roaring
A waterfall falling through the air.

I will put in the box …
Seven special silk wishes
The sound of birds cheeping
The smell of a cake being baked.

I will put in the box …
The smell of a warm fire burning,
And the smell of apple pie,
The sound of an owl hooting.

My box is made of snow
And glimmering gold,
All covered in sprinkling stars.
I will keep it in the sands of ancient Egypt.

Amy Hunter (8)
Kingston St Mary CE Primary School, Taunton

Christmas

C hristmas is fun with family
H aving presents is fun too
R ed robins dancing in the snow
 I ncredible snowflakes flying through the air
S now lying on the ground
T ick-tock, tick-tock goes the big grandfather clock
M mmm, Christmas dinner
A mazing stocking
S now everywhere!

Holly Salter (9)
Kingston St Mary CE Primary School, Taunton

Ye Old Market

(Inspired by the history of Taunton market)

Yesterday's horse waste
Sitting crammed between the cobbles,
With street criers calling out their wares.
Clattering sound of rickety carts
Bumping and rattling along the cobbled street
Into the morning mist,
As the delicious odour of newly-baked bread
Floats along the breeze.
A minor skirmish breaks out near the butcher's.

The sight of blood at the blacksmith's
As he uses pliers to pull out teeth.
You must take care
For nearby residences will pour
Household waste from upstairs windows.

Dost thou still like ye olde market now?

George Clews & Jack Sweet (9)
Kingston St Mary CE Primary School, Taunton

Fire

Fire
Fire burns badly.
Twisty, turny light.
As bright as a red tomato.
As hot as an egg in an egg cup.
I feel scared of fire.
As scared as cooked
Chicken. Fire
Makes me
Think of
Bonfire
Night.

Helena Minnis (9)
Kingston St Mary CE Primary School, Taunton

Fire

Fire
Fire is dangerous.
Golden, flamey, yellow.
As hot as a cooker when it's on.
As golden as a daffodil.
I am afraid of fire -
As afraid as a dog when there're fireworks.
Fire.
Fire makes me think of a sunset.

Kirsten Hancock (9)
Kingston St Mary CE Primary School, Taunton

Stars

S himmering stars light up the sky.
T hey stand out like a flash of gold.
A mazingly they lead the way,
R acing through the sky like angels.

Molly Durrant (9)
Kingston St Mary CE Primary School, Taunton

Fire

Fire
It can burn
Burning, flaming, golden
As hot as the sun
As bright as a light bulb
I am frightened as a baby bird
Fire
Fire is hyper.

Sam Preston (9)
Kingston St Mary CE Primary School, Taunton

Our Playground

Can be sunny and friendly
Happy, noisy and cheerful.
As fun as a fair
As noisy as the birds.
I feel safe and happy
I feel as safe as in my house.
Our playground
Is the best in the world.

Kathryn Littlewood (9)
Kingston St Mary CE Primary School, Taunton

Lunchtime

The birds are chirping in the trees
The flowers, bright and the buzzing bees
The children play rounders in the bright sunshine
Some read books in the shade of the pine.
One family of rabbits run back into their hole
As one little boy miss aims his bowl
A group of girls make daisy chains
The boys all laugh and call them names.
The butterflies scatter from the grass
As the children get called back to class.

Charlotte Jones (11)
La Retraite Swan School, Salisbury

What Is Blue?

Blue makes me think about a saxophone
The water of a lake.
A favourite song about a friend
Or dancing in the wind
In an enchanted forest
With the sun going down.

Christiana Berezin (8)
La Retraite Swan School, Salisbury

Trenches

I can see,
Dead men caught up in
the cruel barbed wire.
Stretching over the unknown land
Tracer bullets flicker over
my head, lighting up
the pitch-black night sky.

I can hear,
the cries of the wounded,
stranded and paralysed
in the middle of
no-man's-land.
The unending sound
of machine gun fire
is overwhelming.

I can feel,
the murky water
surround my legs.
As I walk my feet
sink into the mud.
Loneliness is all
around me.

Oliver Bradshaw (10)
La Retraite Swan School, Salisbury

I Love My Guinea Pig

I love my guinea pig, she is called Hally
It is a girl, we play with her every day
She has a run in our garden
She is a Chinese guinea pig.
I feed her every day
Her coat is orange and white
She is one year old
Her birthday is August 6th.

William Bailey-Hobbs (8)
La Retraite Swan School, Salisbury

Around The Rainforest

In the rainforest are trees
With their great brown trunks
Hear those creaking branches
Feel the scratchy, rough bark
And those tangled roots
That curve everywhere
Home to many creatures.

Under the rainforest are bugs
Scampering everywhere
Avoid their nasty nips
As they try to defend
Hear the buzz of wings
Watch the tiny ants
And bugs with exotic patterns.

Above the rainforest is sunlight
Filtering through the leaves
Observe the stunning light
Destroying the dark shadows
Listen to the rustling of leaves
Feel the warmth of the sun
Cutting through the darkness.

Around the rainforest is life
Beware the lurking predator
Virtually invisible
Watch the tiny insects
Hear the tweeting birds
Feel the beautiful plants
Life is everywhere.

James Cole
La Retraite Swan School, Salisbury

Night

He is nasty,
He is scary and lonely,
He is full of bad dreams,
He is like a fierce burglar.

He has a dark and evil face,
His eyes are horrible and dark,
He has really sharp teeth,
His hair is black and matted.

His clothes are big, baggy and dark,
He is always slithering around like a snake,
He lives in a deep, dark hole,
He makes me very scared and
Makes me sleep.

Imogen Blair (10)
La Retraite Swan School, Salisbury

My Cat

My cat is quite an idiot,
He jumps around all day,
In the summer holidays,
He jumped in a pile of hay.

He really hates the dog down the road,
Especially in May,
Yesterday he walked straight past our house
And the cat simply ran away.

My cat is really stupid,
He ran into a wall today,
This morning he ran straight up to me
And coughed up a mouse called Tay.

Robin Sedden (9)
La Retraite Swan School, Salisbury

Chocolate

Watch it melt in the heat,
Freeze in the cold,
What a tasty treat,
Brown, oblong,
Hard,
Shape.
What more could you wish for?
It's very easy to eat,
Feel it melt in your mouth,
Savour the taste of this special treat!

Lydia Edwards (11)
La Retraite Swan School, Salisbury

What Is White?

White is as soft as a cloud floating by,
Clean as a new piece of paper that stands out,
Ghost sheets, scary!
White is a light feather,
Fresh shirts without stains,
You can count on that!

Alice Pearse (9)
La Retraite Swan School, Salisbury

Autumn

In a haze of silver mist,
Where golden leaves turn and twist,
And wind whispers through the trees
Where sunlight shines and dapples leaves.

Bronze and orange, red and gold,
Flutter to the autumn floor,
And in the morning crystal-clear,
Sparkling frost, goodbye till next year.

Kathryn Hoddinott (11)
La Retraite Swan School, Salisbury

Snow Wolf

His teeth are icicles
Dripping wet
And glinting bright
His coat is gleaming white
Covered in snow
As he howls
The wind howls with him
He runs through the woods
As fast as he can
Whilst the blizzards blow
Heavy with snow
His paws are soft
And silky smooth
Just like the snow
He lives upon.
His eyes are white
As they reflect the snow
That covers the ground
His pupil is a hailstone
Hard and cold
Just like his expression
and breaking heart
He curls up under the trees
And goes into eternal darkness
Until another year.

Sophie Forster (11)
La Retraite Swan School, Salisbury

The Butterfly

I see a beautiful butterfly
Through the sky as bright as the sun,
And it flutters down on a flower
Eating sweet, sweet pollen
As you see!

Elina Ho (8)
La Retraite Swan School, Salisbury

Orlando Bloom

There once was a man called Orli
Who liked being in movies that were gory
He had a new goal
That in his latest role
He would steal one of the Queen's corgis.

There once was a man called Orli
Who one day felt rather poorly
He watched news galore
Labour knocked on his door
'Sorry,' he said, 'I'm Tory.'

There once was a man called Bloom
Who one day sat in the gloom
He watched 'The Office' boxsets
When suddenly all of his pets
Burst through the door with a boom.

There once was a man called Bloom
Who one day visited a tomb
He had the fright of his life
When he saw a huge knife
'You Sir are a buffoon.'

Lucy Robson (11)
La Retraite Swan School, Salisbury

Friends

Friends are always there for you,
So you should be there for them too,
They stand up for you, friends do,
Your face lights up when you're with them,
They always will lend you something if you need it,
Bit by bit
You start to grow apart,
You start to like different things.
You start to move on . . .

Nia Singleton (11)
La Retraite Swan School, Salisbury

Death

Death looks like a room without all the furniture,
Similar to a ghost coming through a window,
Looks like the dark
Draining the light out of you.

Death feels like sand
Falling straight through your fingers,
The same as a million daggers thrown at you,
Rather like a painful prick of a finger.

Death tastes like a mouldy apple,
Brown with spots.
Comparing a fish with green scales,
A gruel all lumpy and grey.

Death is like the First World War
When people were suffering.
Exactly like a diary,
Things which never leave your head,
Quite like an odour that will never go away.

Eva Bryan (9)
La Retraite Swan School, Salisbury

Storm Wolf

The storm wolf prowls through the night's sky
With flashes of lightning passing by.
With a growl he strikes
Descending from the sky come lightning pikes
The storm ends and it is time to die.

The storm wolf waits for its time to rise again
To strike on the awaiting men.
When its time comes it takes the chance
And descends the lightning dance
As the storm wolf enters his waiting den.

Georgina Dollittle (10)
La Retraite Swan School, Salisbury

My Dog Goldie

My dog was sweet,
She seriously loved her meat,
She had fun
Under the blazing sun,
And her name was gorgeous Goldie.

Her beautiful blue eyes,
Reminded me of mine,
She was a gorgeous lass,
The problem is she's in the past,
And she laid herself down to rest.

I can see her up there,
Brave as a bear,
She's seeing me soon,
When the sun lights the moon,
I'll see her in my dreams.

Charlotte Nicol (11)
La Retraite Swan School, Salisbury

My Best Friend

My friend is the best,
She's trendy with her purple vest.
She has long brown hair,
And does really care.
I can trust her wherever I stroll,
And she promises she won't tell a soul.
She has a horse called Kaya,
And she even lets me ride her.
She's always there to say, 'Hi!'
Whenever I need a shoulder to cry.
I really do love her so,
I just hope she'll never go.
Because I need her,
Forever!

Kirsty Ballard (11)
La Retraite Swan School, Salisbury

Mountains

Mountains are pristine teeth,
But nobody knows what lies beneath.
The treasures under all that white,
Strong canines waiting just to bite,
Like a beautiful fan of snow,
Reflecting the sun's rays and glow,
On the side of the mountain.

Round the rocky mountains are bears,
But nobody, no one ever dares
To interrupt them as they eat
Their lunch of luscious animal meat,
The nearby grazing sheep,
Snatching them from the farmer's keep,
On the tip of the mountain.

A very cold, musty atmosphere,
Set points in our earthly sphere
Like stalagmites looking extremely fierce,
Or a fang waiting to pierce,
Shimmering in the strong moonlight,
The light that only comes at night
On the summit of the mountain.

Hannah Webber (10)
La Retraite Swan School, Salisbury

My Best Friend

She's got golden hair
She likes to share
She has blue eyes
And is very wise.
She's there to say, 'Hi!'
And is there when I need to cry.
She's my best friend
Right to the end
She will always be the best.
Kirsty!

Chloe Fooks (11)
La Retraite Swan School, Salisbury

The Motorway

The gleaming colours of the
Cars streaming past me,
Streaming smoke
Like shooting stars.
The rumbling of engines
Shooting past me,
With a rush of air
Like a rocket in space.

The gleam of the sunlight
Beams upon me,
The colours of the cars get
Brighter still.
The fiery sun gets brighter
And brighter,
While the colours of the cars get
More and more bold.

The end of the motorway gets
Closer and closer,
The colours of cars get less
And less.
The gleam of the sunlight
Gets dimmer and dimmer,
And the old city roads
Get more and more dull.

William Sharpe (10)
La Retraite Swan School, Salisbury

The Sunset

I feel the sunset rising on the hill,
I hear the waves splashing on the beach,
I smell fresh strawberries from the market,
I see dolphins jumping in the sea.

Georgia Edwards (8)
La Retraite Swan School, Salisbury

Abandoned

Out in the cold I'm freezing and scared,
I thought he would come as if he cared!
When I was hungry he didn't give me food,
He would push me away when he was in a mood!

Now I'm sitting in this itchy sack,
I'm so cramped I can't scratch my back.
The rain is coming down on my head,
Oh I long to be at home in bed!

What about my friends Whiskers and Bert?
I hope they're OK, I hope they're not hurt.
I know I'm going to be OK
Because I can hear footsteps, it's the RSPCA.

Again I'm with other animals cats, dogs,
Snakes, lizards and bright green frogs!
Everyone wanted me, then a couple phoned,
In a second I was rehomed!

I'm happy now every day,
I can run, hunt and even play.
I'm the happiest cat ever,
I never want to leave this family ever!

Catherine Morrison (10)
La Retraite Swan School, Salisbury

Seasons

Falling leaves, *crunch, crunch, crunch,*
Red holly berries all in a bunch,
Brown, orange, green and red,
Black, yellow, gold on my shed.

Falling leaves, *crunch, crunch, crunch,*
Snap, snap, snap,
All in a bunch,
On the trees,
Off the trees, everywhere!

Jack Killick (9)
La Retraite Swan School, Salisbury

D-Day

I can see the swirling planes
Zooming in the sky.
The gunfire of the infantry,
Men killing the enemy like sudden death.
The tanks moving to their destination
On the darkened sand.
The dead people on the ground
Like people without graves.

I can hear the gunfire
Like an animal ready to kill its prey.
The people crying for help
On the ground as they get shot
Like electric dolls out of control.
The patter of the rain falls on me.
The squelching of the mud
On the ground as we step forward.

I can feel anger for the
People who started the war.
Fear is among us
Because we might die any second.
The rain dripping on my head.
Love for the people who are dead,
Who did nothing to deserve it.

Hugh McLean (10)
La Retraite Swan School, Salisbury

My Favourite Things

I wish I had a year-time's supply of chocolate,
I'd share it with me and my mate,
I would have a limo to take me to Cadbury Land every day
And I'd get my mum and dad to pay,
Me and my uncle would get really fat
And we'd have a heart attack on my mat.

Molly Cook (11)
La Retraite Swan School, Salisbury

Horses

Black are their hooves,
Lumps of black coal.
Tack on their backs,
Snakes slithering along.

Brown are their eyes,
Clay painted brown.
Hair on their head,
Pieces of brown string.

Cream are their bodies,
Vanilla ice cream.
Noses that sneeze
Like cottage cheese.

Silver are their stirrups,
Dew on the grass.
Name tags that shine,
Tears on my face.

Gold are their hearts,
The sun in the sky.
Sun in their eyes,
A king's golden crown.

Caroline Attard (9)
La Retraite Swan School, Salisbury

My Garden

My garden can be whatever you want it to be,
It will suit your mood any day of the week,
It can be like a bright picture,
Or like a rainy day, whichever will make you relax and stay.
When I am in my garden I want to be there forever.
On opening the door,
It's like a huge rainbow,
In a bright blue sky.
In my garden you will never be alone,
You will have the birds singing all around.

Alice Bowen (9)
La Retraite Swan School, Salisbury

Love Is Beautiful

I've never felt this way before,
It's a warm feeling galore,
Why do I feel this way?
I've never had such a wonderful day.

It sounds like flowing music,
It tastes like something sweet,
It smells like roses in full bloom,
It looks like birds going tweet, tweet.

It reminds me when I was little
With my mum so fair,
I used to cuddle up to her
When I had a scare.

This is what I know,
I love this person so,
I really think we could have it all,
We could have a family and be happy because
Love is beautiful.

Jessica Webber (9)
La Retraite Swan School, Salisbury

Elephants

They feel crinkly, wrinkly and definitely not soft
And if you think that's bad you should taste them.
If you've smelt manure, that's an elephant smell.
They're so loud you think your ears are popping.
Elephants look so big, you just have to scream.

Does it matter if they aren't all pretty
Or if their nose is too long?
If elephants don't want to look ravishing
Why should they have to put perfume on
Or get plastic surgery on their noses?
And as for looking big and scary
That's a load of nonsense too!

Stephanie Davey (10)
La Retraite Swan School, Salisbury

War

Swirling planes like eagles flying overhead.
I can see fires with melting faces in them
Like the flames from Hell.
Soldiers dying and losing hearts
Like a shot rabbit killed by a hunter.
Guns firing making men fall.

I can hear wounded soldiers crying for help,
A gun with a repetitive sound that won't stop
And makes a rat-ta-tat-tat sound,
The squelching of the mud being squashed
And squelching like crushing a man,
Men shouting with aggression like a ferocious lion.

I can feel the rain pouring down
And giving me sadness.
The mud in the trenches squelching on my feet
Like a dead man with no bones.
The agony from a bullet gives me no chance
Of surviving like a bird with a broken wing.

Nicholas Finlayson (10)
La Retraite Swan School, Salisbury

The Earth Gets Destroyed

Meteors burn, glow and smash,
Comets freeze bright at night,
Asteroids smash, bash and mash,
Global dimming decreases light.

Tsunami flood and cover people in mud,
Global warming boils meat,
Volcanoes cover people in lava colour of blood,
Earthquakes break pipes which makes heat!

Black holes swallow everything in sight,
Martians invade in the dead of night!

William Garston (9)
La Retraite Swan School, Salisbury

The Rainbow

Green looks like a meadow,
In a nearby field.

Pink as the cleanest pig
In town.

Blue is like water waving
To you on the beach.

Yellow as butter slipping
Through your fingers.

Red is like the only
Red rose in the garden.

White like a snowdrop
In the dead still winter.

Black is dark as a dog
At night.

A rainbow is as beautiful
As anything.

Chloe David (10)
La Retraite Swan School, Salisbury

What Is Brown?

Birds' feathers are brown,
Gloomy, dark and mysterious.
It's a tail of a lion,
Gravy on your Christmas dinner.
Reminding you of wood.
Hair like the bark of a tree,
Or chocolate melting in your hand.
Old stained glass windows,
Liquid from the science room.
School doors are brown,
So are hedgehogs and rabbits,
Horses and rats too!

James Bold (9)
La Retraite Swan School, Salisbury

Lions

The lion is the king of all animals,
He sounds like it too.
Don't get in his way while he's hunting,
Or you'll be his meal, unlucky for you.

He looks like a huge fur ball,
He feels like it too.
He lives where the grass is tall,
But not as high as you.

He smells like he needs a bath,
He's not as tall as a giraffe,
But he's still big enough to see
Where the antelope will be.

It's time for me to go now,
So goodbye to you,
Watch out for the lions,
They're coming for you.

Molly Viner (10)
La Retraite Swan School, Salisbury

My Pony Stew

Stew neighed,
His tail swayed
As he galloped through the grass.
He looks like a blurred painting
When he goes that fast.

Stew has a kind nature
So we took him to a show,
But at the starting line he thought of food
Then he wouldn't go.

When we went home I bet he was thinking
Whoo I didn't get a beating,
I put him in his stable,
Although I was only just able.

Emma Peacey (10)
La Retraite Swan School, Salisbury

Fire

I can see your colours
Gleaming in the air.
Seeing your untamed flame
Growing higher, wider through the sky.

Your spiky image
Is the twilight of the sky.
I can see the light
Of your beauty.

Hearing your roar,
Your ear piercing crackle,
Ear-deafening explosions
And I can hear you move.

You flay around,
Screaming all the time.
I can hear you flying through the air,
You sound like a roaring beast.

Feeling your heat,
Is like feeling death.
Your pain is indescribable,
All I feel is pain.

Jordan Griffiths (10)
La Retraite Swan School, Salisbury

My Dog

I love my dog because he is lively and cute.
He feels like a new cuddly toy.
He smells as if he has just come out of water
And been dried.
My dog looks like a pile of black fluff.
He barks like a guard dog,
But deep down inside
He would not hurt a fly.
My dog reminds me of my bed.

Lindsey Budd (10)
La Retraite Swan School, Salisbury

Colours

Red is anger burning your face,
Or blood oozing out of a cut
Or a fresh apple on a tree.

Blue is sad and emotional,
Soothing and sleepy,
Or an ocean.

Yellow is a happy summer's day,
A creative painting,
Or a fun day out.

Green is an exciting day,
Telling you go!
Go have fun.

Gold is rich,
Wealth is changing you,
Or moving you.

Silver is a beautiful night,
A shining moon or star,
A spirit of the night.

Diamond is a stunning star,
Beauty shining in the night,
Fantastic light glittering all night.

Patrick Ba-Tin (10)
La Retraite Swan School, Salisbury

What Is Lilac?

Lilac is the colour of peace,
Like a fairground in a field.
Lilac reminds me of tulips.
Lilac is summer - happy and glorious.
Lilac is like a wonderful dream.
Lilac is like a wedding dress.
Lavender and its sweet smell are lilac.
Lilac is a gardener smiling at the world.

Victoria Davey (8)
La Retraite Swan School, Salisbury

Space

The shining stars that surround me,
Clouds the sea and land on Earth.
A sun that is expanding,
Its flames like a trapped animal.
The rocky floor of the planet,
With footprints made by my follower.

A rustling coldness in my bones,
But also happiness of being here.
A sadness of not being at home,
But now slipping on the rocky floor that is crumbling beneath,
I feel as light as a feather and I could fly forever.

A thump of the ground,
Swishing of the shooting star.
Burning of the monstrous sun,
My spaceship calling to go back.

Jordan Neale (10)
La Retraite Swan School, Salisbury

If I Ruled The World

If I ruled the world there wouldn't be school,
We would be too busy in our pools.
Parents would be cool,
They would call my brother a fool.

If I ruled the world there would be loads of ponies,
So no one would be lonely.
There would be a water park in Newton Tony
And it would be for girls only.

If I ruled the world kids would cook the food
Then everyone would be in a good mood.
Poodles' legs would not be nude,
Adults could not do anything, their hands would be superglued.

Laura Hollingbery (9)
La Retraite Swan School, Salisbury

What Is Blue?

Blue is the sea when the waves are rough.
Blue is for drinking when you're out of puff.
It is a beautiful flower called forget-me-nots.
Blue is for writing with.
It's the sky when it is warm and sunny.
It is the clothes that you wear and the shoes too.
Blue is for the books that we read.
It is a beautiful lagoon.
You can use it for a colour of pencil case
Or a poster for decoration.
It's to use on a flag or paper.
Blue violets can make a good smell.
Blue is the best,
'Wonderful', I would say.
Blue is quite cold,
No doubt about that.

Elizabeth Morgan (9)
La Retraite Swan School, Salisbury

The Toilet Brush Monster

The toilet brush ate my mum, whilst I was out at play,
I really thought I heard her scream, when I was on my way.
It did not make a difference though,
For she was down with flu.
I loved it when she bought me things,
Lovely and brand new.

This monster feels like gooey slime,
He is like a walking crime.
In here there are tiny mice,
Which look like little grains of rice.

Help get me out of here!

Olivia Wilson (10)
La Retraite Swan School, Salisbury

D-Day June 6th, 1944

Today might be my last day as I could be shot.
I can see the scared soldiers running for their lives.
I can see the guns being fired at
Whilst the bombs are exploding.
Planes passing by in the midnight sky.

I can feel the muddy footsteps of a scared soldier
Which could lead you to your death.
I can feel the bombs
And guns swooping by in a scared way,
But take care as anything can happen.

I can hear all of the planes passing by,
They will be dropping bombs
Which could decide your fate.
But anything can happen
And it could even happen to you.

Clive Marcus (11)
La Retraite Swan School, Salisbury

The Savannah

The lion is gold in the sun,
Its crouching body is like a mound of sand,
Still as a building, but ready to pounce,
Laying under the tree shadows casting mystical shapes on its back.

The sound of the guinea fowl calling out, warning each other,
A sound of breaking twigs from the impala,
The wind blown in the trees and with it the scent of the prey,
Silence broken by the almighty roar from the distant lion.

The hard hoofs of the wildebeest trampled over the spiky thorns,
The hot day pounded down on the animals,
A cool breeze flowed across the grass giving a cold sensation,
The dry mud broken beneath your feet and the cracks crumbled away.

James Martin (10)
La Retraite Swan School, Salisbury

Trenches

Rotting bodies in the mud,
Rats scuttling around you,
Exploding bombs throwing up clay,
Comrades around you rotting away,
The dirt a murky brown.

Bits of shrapnel flying everywhere,
Planes soaring around you,
Soldiers marching up and down the lines,
Less and less come back,
The mire a murky brown.

The sound of men crying out,
The thud as they hit the ground,
Men marching in the mud,
A machine gun firing up,
The click of the gun reloading.

I feel myself sink lower and lower
Into the thick brown mud,
I shake all over,
A bomb hits the ground,
The ice cold water
Trickles down my back.

The sound of a bullet hits me,
I fall to the ground,
My mates shout at me
To see if I'm alright,
I hear the grunt of the doctor
Carrying me on a stretcher.

The noise of the ambulance
Taking me to hospital,
The nurse is hurrying around in a warm room.

Theo Daniel (10)
La Retraite Swan School, Salisbury

Winter Poem

I step out into the bitter air
And face what's in front of me.
Snowmen and snowballs
All around the streets.
I step out with my spade
To dig the driveway free.
Then the snow hits the tree
And the last living leaf falls.
I sit down at the right time
To dodge a misplaced snowball.
Then I turn to see,
Somebody is copying me.
It's Mr Smith from down the road,
Doing what he needs to do.

George Sharpe (9)
La Retraite Swan School, Salisbury

What Is Black?

Black is dangerous.
Liquorice.
Black is a bold black knight fighting the wrath,
It is the darkness, a black silky bed,
Sometimes it is warm and sometimes it is cold.
Black is an old abandoned castle
Waiting for finders.
It is a bin liner and a bin.
Sometimes even writing on a page
Or on a video tape.
Black is for hair, the fur on your head.
Black is mean and unforgiving,
There is no doubt about that.

William Hoddinott (9)
La Retraite Swan School, Salisbury

What Is Lilac?

Lilac is warm, soothing and calm.
Forget-me-nots blowing in the wind.
When cold think lilac,
Get warm quick.
You go lilac when holding your breath,
The same as the mountains in the distance.
Lilac is slow, quiet and lovely,
Loving and shy.
This is lilac,
Do you like it?

Oscar Treleaven (9)
La Retraite Swan School, Salisbury

What Is Green?

Green is a leaf
Shining in the light.
Green is felt and sometimes card,
It is grass and fields as well.
Broccoli lies dark on my plate.
Green is for a cover on a book,
It is all around us,
Cars are sometimes green.

Harry Hart (9)
La Retraite Swan School, Salisbury

Balloon Haiku

Balloons soaring high
Microscopic city there
Shapes over Bristol.

Spencer Ford (9)
Longwell Green Primary School, Bristol

Balloons Haikus

Floating high balloons
Peaceful, gliding, calm, high views
Sensational sky.

Microscopic shapes
Colourful scenery there
Extremely big heights.

Like rainbow colours
Sensational, beautiful
Soaring, high balloons.

Jacob Miller (9)
Longwell Green Primary School, Bristol

Look Around You

A rabbit hops,
A balloon pops.
A lion roars,
A footballer snores.
The flower smells,
The church rings its bells.
The spider spins a web.

Jessica Dudley (10)
Longwell Green Primary School, Bristol

A Hot Air Balloon Haikus

I want to go up
In a big hot air balloon
Up, up, up, so high!

I took off, away
What amazing fun to have
Boy, it is so high!

Aaron Gough (9)
Longwell Green Primary School, Bristol

Soaring Haiku

Soaring through the air
Are beautiful views to see
Colours on balloons.

Yasmin Shirmanesh (9)
Longwell Green Primary School, Bristol

Me In My Hot Air Balloon Haiku

Flying my balloon
Seeing colourful balloons
All beautiful scenes.

Hannah Tapscott (8)
Longwell Green Primary School, Bristol

Bristol Balloons Haiku

Beautiful balloons
Soaring high over Bristol
It's sensational.

Joshua Munday (9)
Longwell Green Primary School, Bristol

The Balloon Ride Haiku

A balloon floating
Soars through the colourful sky
A peaceful balloon.

Corey Reid (9)
Longwell Green Primary School, Bristol

The Balloon Ride! Haiku

The hot air balloon
Gliding very peacefully
Then comes the landing!

Rachel Lim (8)
Longwell Green Primary School, Bristol

Balloons Haiku

Soaring in the sky,
The view is very quiet,
Then comes the landing!

Charlotte Hawley (9)
Longwell Green Primary School, Bristol

A Balloon Haiku

Up, up in the sky,
A wonderful sensation,
The cars look like ants.

Isabel Daone (9)
Longwell Green Primary School, Bristol

Flying In A Balloon! Haiku

Hovering around
Having a great time flying
Without any sound.

Anna Clark (9)
Longwell Green Primary School, Bristol

The Balloon Haiku

Microscopic town
Beautiful, colourful sky,
Relaxing, scenic.

Daniel Davies (9)
Longwell Green Primary School, Bristol

In A Hot Balloon Haiku

Nervous going up
Hot air balloons gliding high
Amazing view there.

Jack Williams (8)
Longwell Green Primary School, Bristol

The Balloon Ride Haiku

Balloons look calming
High balloons are beautiful
With peaceful colours.

Joshua Collins (8)
Longwell Green Primary School, Bristol

In A Hot Air Balloon Haiku

My dad's balloon flight
He could see everything
Until landing . . . bump!

Shannon Ponter (9)
Longwell Green Primary School, Bristol

A Balloon Ride Haiku

A really high view
Feels like gliding like a bird
Following the flock.

Ben Clapp (9)
Longwell Green Primary School, Bristol

A Hot Air Balloon Haiku

What peaceful gliding!
Shapes and sizes, what a view!
All different colours.

Thomas George (9)
Longwell Green Primary School, Bristol

Balloons Haiku

A really high view
Up in a hot air balloon
Everything is small.

Jason Granville (8)
Longwell Green Primary School, Bristol

What's Scary About A Balloon? Haiku

Guess what is scary?
The scary bit is landing,
So get out and quick!

Ella Hicken (8)
Longwell Green Primary School, Bristol

Friends

Friends are good,
Friends are fun,
Friends will play with everyone.

Friends are good,
Friends are fun,
Friends like playing in the sun.

I like friends,
Friends are fun,
Friends are everything a girl could want.

Lucy Gazzard (9)
Longwell Green Primary School, Bristol

The Balloon Ride Haiku

Spectacular view
Hovering over Bristol
Swaying in the breeze.

Mitchell Thornton (9)
Longwell Green Primary School, Bristol

The Balloon Ride! Haiku

Bristol is peaceful
With a sensational view
Brunel's famous bridge.

Elliott Gibbons (9)
Longwell Green Primary School, Bristol

Horses Kennings

Tail whacker
Show jumper
Easy catcher
Foot printer
Horse jumper
Bad moulter
Groom liker
Competition winner
Noise hater
Grass eater
Hay muncher
Fox disliker
White canterer
Horse dancer
Play fighter
Horse bucker
Happy hunter.

Hannah Adams (10)
Lydeard St Lawrence School, Taunton

Pony Kennings

Big jumper
Tail whacker
Groom licker
Breeding leader
Happy muncher
Galloping galloper
Horse dancer
Trotting pouncer
Loving roller
Vegetable eater
Grass lover
Jumping bouncer.

Rebecca Down (9)
Lydeard St Lawrence School, Taunton

The Cheetah Kennings

Fast runner
Tree climber
Forest blurrer
Flesh hunter.

Speed maker
Food stalker
Meat eater
Blood seeker.

Antelope catcher
African predator
Lithe slayer
Weakness spotter.

Speckled assassin
Camouflaged cheetah
Spotted carnivore
Animal biter.

William McColl (9)
Lydeard St Lawrence School, Taunton

Cow Kennings

Muck maker
Shed hater
Tail wagger
Milk donator
Beef provider
Silage grabber
Hay muncher
Grass cruncher
Spotty runner
Deafening mooer
Ear pointer.

Daniel Sinkins (10)
Lydeard St Lawrence School, Taunton

Bats Kennings

Fruit eater
Night-time streaker.

Insect muncher
Gnat cruncher.

Noise maker
Risk taker.

Dark flyer
Quick flyer.

Daytime sleeper
Night creeper.

Sonic hearer
Prey getting nearer.

Cave sneaker
Food keeper.

Neck chewer
Blood remover.

Josh Newman (11)
Lydeard St Lawrence School, Taunton

Cats Kennings

Fur licker
Fun tickler
Mice catcher
Bad scratcher
House runner
Ball lover
Big jumper
Clever climber
Mud bringer
Dog merry maker
Sofa ripper
Night watcher
Mouse attacker
Noise breaker
Sound rapper
Wasp killer
Water spiller
Time taker
Food muncher
Bird taker.

Drummond Kesson Ross (10)
Lydeard St Lawrence School, Taunton

Guess Who? Kennings

Ocean dweller
Ice breaker
Water lover
Big discoverer
Sea dancer
Beauty entrancer
Human taker
Long liver
Strong singer
Storm shaker
Peace maker.

Ocean ruler
Wave basher
Coral smasher
Wise leader
Huge feeder
Plankton eater
Silent sleeper
Nosy parker
Long migrator.

Blue whale!

Alice Baldwin
Lydeard St Lawrence School, Taunton

Bear Kennings

Tree breaker
Body tearer
Meat eater
Loud roarer
Forest dweller
Muscle builder
Hair wearer
Big bloater
Blood hunter
Death seeker
Brain sucker
Quiet hibernator
Animal catcher
Man muncher
Branch crusher
Flesh wanter
Child carer
Baby protector
Fear maker
Gut gobbler . . .

Guess who?
A bear!

Laurence Ryan (10)
Lydeard St Lawrence School, Taunton

Rabbit Kennings

Hole miner
Thistle eater
Food whiner
Friendly greeter.

High jumper
Quiet talker
Fur dumper
Fast walker.

Ear wibbler
Child delighter
Dandelion nibblers
Quick fighter.

Carrot cruncher
Flea itcher
Grass muncher
Whisker twitcher.

Patrick Greenway (9)
Lydeard St Lawrence School, Taunton

Guess Who? Kennings

Tail drooper
Extra super

Floor basher
Food smasher

Floor sweeper
High leaper

Cat seeker
Bone weeper

Hole digger
Funny snigger

Shoe wrecker
Ball getter.

Guess who?
A dog.

Megan Morley (10)
Lydeard St Lawrence School, Taunton

Cow Kennings

Field grazer
Curious gazer
Cake cruncher
Hay muncher
Mooing narrator
Milk creator
Calf carer
Bedding tearer
Escape darer
Black and white wearer
Tail swisher
Buttercup wisher
Mooching walker
Lush grass stalker
Peace tracer
Peace facer.

Elly Greenway (11)
Lydeard St Lawrence School, Taunton

Dog Kennings

Dad disliker
Supreme striker
Mum minder
Bird finder
Dove scarer
Food scoffer
Never offer.

Aidan R Johnson (10)
Lydeard St Lawrence School, Taunton

My Dog Kennings

Meat eater
Rat hunter
Mouse killer
Cow chaser
Feet warmer
Bark maker
Fast runner
Long jumper
Food lover
Cat hater
Bad biter
Toy breaker
Sweet motherer
Early waker
Peace bringer
Bad fighter.

Tansy Purdey (10)
Lydeard St Lawrence School, Taunton

Kitten Kennings

Friendly moulter
Tree climber
Black lapper
Speedy spiller
Rat poker
Bird chaser
Mouse killer
Dog attacker
Paw printer.

Rhys Walker (9)
Lydeard St Lawrence School, Taunton

Dog Kennings

Paw licker
Sock stealer
Cat hater
Hole digger
Rat disliker
Hopeless jumper
Tail wagger
Toe tickler
Fast runner
Bottom licker
Ball chaser
Mouse eater
Food finisher
Puddle maker
Quick swimmer
Boy lover.

Guy Penny (9)
Lydeard St Lawrence School, Taunton

Ferret Kennings

Finger nibbler
Rabbit killer
Arm scratcher
Teeth grower
Good murderer
Food scavenger
Hole digger
Wood chewer
Fast runner
Long sleeper
Unique smeller
Night creeper
Rat shifter
Sharp hearer
Quiet crawler.

Robert Gribble (11)
Lydeard St Lawrence School, Taunton

Cat Kennings

Ginger runner
Miaow crier
High jumper
Tree climber
Whisker measurer
Eye glower
Human attracter
Bag ripper
Speed shifter
Milk sipper
Blood sniffer
Claw digger
Bird sniper
Rat trickster
Rabbit crippler
Mouse terminator.

Sarah Spiller (10)
Lydeard St Lawrence School, Taunton

Dog Kennings

Black and white runner
Cat chaser
Rat catcher
Hole digger

Mum minder
Sheep worker
Ball player
Guard keeper

Nose smeller
Bone burier
Rabbit catcher
Tail wagger.

Samantha Gridley (10)
Lydeard St Lawrence School, Taunton

Guess Who? Kennings

Noise maker
Ride taker
Gallop racer
Hoof pacer
Horse talker
Fast walker
Show jumper
Shoe clumper
Grass muncher
Hay cruncher
Chestnut trotter
Self spotter
Ear listener
Tail swisher
Day walker
Stable snoozer . . .
A pony.

Alice Baker (11)
Lydeard St Lawrence School, Taunton

Rat Kennings

Rabbit hater
Cat disliker
Noise squeaker
Small eater
Cheese snatcher
House crawler
Computer controller
Quick runner
Hole dweller.

James Goodman (11)
Lydeard St Lawrence School, Taunton

Alphabet Poem

A ny
B oy
C an
D igest or
E at
F ood
G ulping
H amburgers,
I mportant
J am
K eeps for a
L ong time.
M icro
N uggets,
O h no!
P lease pass a bucket
Q uick - I'm going to be sick!
R ush now, clean it up,
S it still, be quiet.
T im stop chatting
U ntil the end of the day.
V ery good, now how about some
W inning
'X pert
Y ellow
Z zzzzzzz. Tango with mango.

Hannah Price (10)
Mead Vale Primary School, Weston-super-Mare

Spirit

A lonely spirit in the air
B ut not even his parents really
C ared
D ave was his name he never
E ver hurt anyone
F or no one really took the time to
G et to know him
H e hated his life
I was there at the very end seeing him
J umping off the big cliff
K icking, screaming, calling for help
L aunching himself to a horrible death
M any have been bullied but
N ot like this
O ur school bully drove him to his end
P eople cry, whimper and shout
Q uarrelling with others.
'R evenge on bully Carl, he must pay,
S omeone must stop this!'
T his is the day Dave died
U nderground his body lies
V ague memories of the tragic death
W e will never give in to this bully
'X treme action will be taken or
Y ou might be next in the
Z oo of bullied deaths.

Stefan Richards (11)
Mead Vale Primary School, Weston-super-Mare

Bullying

I am Bob the bully
Keep away from me
I might call you names
Or hurt you physically

I am Bob the bully
I beat you up for fun
My friends think it's cool
I think you had better run!

I am Bob the bully
Where has everyone gone?
They've all disappeared
I probably won't find one!

I am Bob the bully
Look at what I've done
I've hurt a lot of children
All just for fun.

Benjamin Gutsell (11)
Mead Vale Primary School, Weston-super-Mare

Happiness Is . . .

Happiness is when you don't have to go to school,
Happiness is when you go on holiday,
Happiness is when it's your birthday,
Happiness is the nice warm summer,
Happiness is when you're not with your teachers,
Happiness is celebrating the joy of Christmas,
Happiness is getting what you want when you want it,
Happiness is having a water fight when it's hot,
Happiness is winning something you wanted to win,
Happiness is when you go to a theme park.

Eleanor Tunnicliffe (10)
Mead Vale Primary School, Weston-super-Mare

My Tree House

I love being in my tree house
my mum and dad can never get me down.
Why? Maybe because I forgot a ladder so when
I get down I have a simple but brilliant way.
Only the masters of the world
would think of this.
You drop!
A
a
a
a
a
h
h
h
crash!

Joshua Smart (10)
Mead Vale Primary School, Weston-super-Mare

Haikus

The Cat
Beside a fireside
White coloured back facing up
Timidly stretching.

The Moon
One glinting crystal
Gazing happily around
Night light in the sky.

Sam Casey (11)
Mead Vale Primary School, Weston-super-Mare

Seaside Shape Poem

The
Waves are
Beating on the
Shore, swirling diving and
S
P
L
A
S
H
I
N
G
Fishermen cast in their nets, splishing, splashing, sploshing
Children paddle in the water, laughing, playing, splashing
Building sandcastles, having fun, jumping gazing but . . .
Smiling!

Olivia Sandys (9)
Mead Vale Primary School, Weston-super-Mare

Haikus

The Moon
One glowing diamond
Sitting on a sheet of black
Lost behind darkness.

The Cat
Sneaking, catching mice
Curled up by the blazing heat
Sly in the moonlight.

Charlotte Balcombe (10)
Mead Vale Primary School, Weston-super-Mare

Haikus

The Cat
Stretching and purring,
A silky, naughty glider,
One glance and she's gone!

The Moon
A shining crystal,
A beautiful, sparkling sphere,
In the velvet sky.

Sophie Bishop-Hurman (11)
Mead Vale Primary School, Weston-super-Mare

Football Fanatic

Football, football you know the rule,
Support your team because they rule!
If the ball's flat or if it's pumped up,
It doesn't matter, we'll win the cup!

Joe Edwards (10)
Mead Vale Primary School, Weston-super-Mare

Haikus

The Cat
Prowling everywhere,
One naughty, frisky kitten,
Eyes beam through dark nights.

The Moon
One silver crystal,
Silently moving near me,
Sailing between clouds.

Stephanie Clark (10)
Mead Vale Primary School, Weston-super-Mare

Haikus

The Moon
One silver crystal
Gazing through my dark bedroom
A glowing night light.

The Cat
Two green glowing eyes
Pouncing at the cautious prey
Creeping through the dark.

Amber Morris (11)
Mead Vale Primary School, Weston-super-Mare

Haikus

The Moon
One beautiful moon
As great as the sun can be
As bright as ten stars.

Cats
Ginger, tabby cats
Prowling through the alleyways
Stalking snoozing mice.

Curtis Dowdell (11)
Mead Vale Primary School, Weston-super-Mare

Fire

F ire is like a red and yellow blob
I think the fire is very hot
R oaring through the petrol
E nding as ashes.

Jordan Puddy (10)
Mead Vale Primary School, Weston-super-Mare

Haikus

The Cat
Found near a fireside,
Ginger gold reflected glow,
Stretch, purr, drift to sleep.

The Moon
One silver crystal,
Silently watching the Earth,
Bringing peace to night.

Jessica Durant (11)
Mead Vale Primary School, Weston-super-Mare

Haikus

The Cat
Glowing slitted eyes
Sharp, pointy, vicious talons
It's in for the kill.

The Moon
The silver crescent
Is like shimmering crystal
Shining upon me.

Lucy Dennis (10)
Mead Vale Primary School, Weston-super-Mare

Family Poem

Dad is lazy and reads the paper all the time
He squeezes citrus fruits like lemon and lime.
He sometimes reads about crime
But his poetry does not rhyme.

Mum is like a chef but she uses a cookery book
She never puts coats on a hook.
Her work is in North Haven brook
And she likes to read a book.

Alex plays with kites
And likes going to different sites.
He doesn't know his left or right
When he does his homework he uses a light.

I'm sneaky and pull off plums from the tree
But sometimes I'm stung by a bumblebee.
I have vegetables for tea
And I like rowing boats in the sea.

Matthew Harvey (8)
Overndale School, Bristol

Family Poem

My mum is very, very good
Usually she makes chocolate pud.
She buys lots of things for me
And she's never late for tea.

My dad is always there for me
Sometimes he forgets his key.
He's really quite good
At making shelves out of wood.

My brother is very cool
He's nearly left school.
He's my only brother
He's even better than my mother.

I climb up the conker tree
I sneak around the apple tree.
Sometimes I take the binoculars off the table
To go to Granny's and check the stable.

Jack Harris (8)
Overndale School, Bristol

My Family Poem

My dad is really cool
He makes the best tea
And his phone always rings
He gives me lots of things.

My mum is good at hard work
She takes me everywhere I want
She is definitely the best
And I will give her a rest.

There is very, very naughty me
I sneak around the apple tree
I am very lazy
I always pick a daisy.

My sister is alright
She is sometimes annoying
She really loves the swimming pool
She is a tiny bit cool.

Katie Bennett (8)
Overndale School, Bristol

My Family Poem

My mum is very cool,
She has lots to say,
Me and mum like the pool,
In the sunshine we shall lay.

My dad is very, very busy,
We have fun every day,
He is making me feel dizzy,
Especially in sunny May.

Dan is my only brother,
He is older than me,
We have lots of fun together,
Sometimes we try to catch a bee.

Holly is my older sister,
She is my only one,
When she went on holiday I missed her,
She puts my hair in a bun.

My name is Kerry,
My best friend's name is Chessy,
Some people call me Cherry,
I am a little bit messy!

Kerry-Dee Shaw (10)
Overndale School, Bristol

My Family Poem

My dad is very kind,
He's very nice and cool
And he likes lots of beer,
Especially when he's watching 'Top Gear'.

My mum is extremely cool,
My mum works at my school,
My mum's very kind,
But she chases me up the stairs.

Charlotte is my older sister,
Charlotte is very nice.
She sometimes lets me in her room,
She tells me off if I make a loud boom.

In the middle of the children it's me
And I'm very annoying,
With my sisters I make up a song,
We like to end it with a bang.

Last but by no means least,
There's Georgie the little one,
She is quite a bit funny,
But she's as cute as a bunny.

Francesca Causon (10)
Overndale School, Bristol

Family Poem

Livia gives me cuddles,
Together we jump in puddles.
Livia likes the swimming pool,
My sister Livia is cool.

My mum likes to spoil me,
She cooks my favourite tea.
She thinks I am funny,
When I am ill I call her Mummy.

Then there's Nick, he's funny,
He treats me like a bunny,
He likes to play jokes,
He always likes to poke.

When my dad hangs out with his mates,
Dad and his mates are always late.
Dad always has a pint of beer,
Lisa says, 'Get into gear.'

Chocoholic is what I am,
My favourite meat is lamb.
I really love art,
My mum says I have a soft heart.

Maddie Hopkinson-Buss (9)
Overndale School, Bristol

Family Poem

I really love my mum
And she is never dumb.
She really likes a daisy
But is sometimes lazy.

I like my dad
He is not bad.
He likes watching football
He is very, very tall.

Ellie is my older sister
She hasn't got a blister.
Ellie has a horse
She rides it, of course.

I am her younger brother
But I want another.
I love my PlayStation
And I'm getting an education.

Lawrence Luffman (9)
Overndale School, Bristol

A Class Six Literacy Lesson

Nobody paying much attention,
knowing if they don't they get detention.
Girls swapping gossip that is irrelevant,
while our teacher's explaining how to spell elephant.
Boys look at their teacher, of whom they are fond,
while infants examine the frog-filled pond.
Hooray, hooray lunchtime at last,
the lesson looks like a thing of the past.

Nicola Pope (11)
Ramsbury Primary School, Marlborough

Lunchtime Play

Rushing down the hallway,
Like a herd of elephants,
Mean people shout, 'Make way!'
Pushing and shoving,
To get there first,
Others wait who are loving.

Hooray today we are on the field,
Like an army going to battle.
The school trample up the hill,
Like angry cattle.

The girls huddle in a quiet corner,
Exchanging the latest gossip,
Some more adventurous,
Go exploring the equipment,
While dinner ladies shout, 'Stop it!'

Boys cover the football pitch,
Trying hard to defeat the rival team,
Kicking each other while tackling,
They really are keen.

Now the bell has rung,
Girls emerge from their quiet spot,
Where they have happily sung,
Boys plod over to line up,
Whilst covered in mud and muck.

Everyone goes down for lessons,
Till the end of the day,
Boo, not hooray!

Sophie Scott (10)
Ramsbury Primary School, Marlborough

Lunchtime

Delicious,
loud,
fun lunchtime.

The boys scoff down their lunches,
then go jabber, jabber,
as they impatiently wait,
to get out into the playground or field
whilst the girls elegantly eat their lunches
also chatting at the same time.

Everyone's now allowed to go out.
They charge,
like two ferocious armies
charging at each other.

Out at last.
The boys make their pitches on the field,
they make their teams and begin.
Goal!
They run around madly shouting
and pumping their fists into the air.
The girls just sit in the shelters
and play truth or dare,
or even just play clapping games.

Deafening,
the bell has rung.
The boys moan and groan,
as they have to go into the dreaded school.
Whereas the girls happily skip into the school,
as they get ready to learn again,
with their teacher.

Sad,
annoyed boys,
happy girls,
end of lunchtime.

Andrew Bethwaite (11)
Ramsbury Primary School, Marlborough

Evil Lunchtime!

The roar of the children rushing out of the classroom,
staking their territory of the dinner hall,
not knowing every step closer to the dinner hall is doom,
when the fat dinner ladies ban balls!

The infants plodding along not knowing when they will go home,
so they will see what evil is among them when they're all alone.

The teachers drinking their tea,
just waiting for the bell to be rung,
every second they're needing a wee,
because they have drunk too much tea.

Lunchtime gets worse when the big, fat, sumo dinner ladies
come up to the field and sit on every child
squashing their bodies and crushing their every tiny little bone
like they're something from the wild.

Finally lunchtime has finished, the horrid threat has gone,
but wait, we now have to go back into the miserable school,
where every living child has to suffer the torture and misery
of the dreaded teachers, who pin you to the wall . . .

Charlie Butler (11)
Ramsbury Primary School, Marlborough

Animals to Ten

One ogre offending others,
Two tanned toads tobogganing together,
Three tough tigers travel treacherously,
Four flabbergasted fish flapping furiously,
Five frantic frogs frolic fabulously,
Six sweet songbirds somersault simultaneously,
Seven secretive snakes slither slyly,
Eight eager eagles elaborate enormously,
Nine negligent newts neglect new nectar,
Ten taunted tadpoles turn to the throne.

Jessica Dixon (11)
Ramsbury Primary School, Marlborough

School Dinners

Roast potatoes
On my plate,
Teachers gossip
All through break.
Milk is all they have
To quaff,
Yet I think
It might be off.
And still they try to
Poison us,
With hamburgers
Covered in puss!
Strange as it is,
We children laugh!
The dinner ladies
Poison us!

Let's see:
Mushy peas
Stuffed with fleas,
Crispy bacon
With soggy croutons,
Jelly that's cold
Is covered with mould!
No wonder we are
Always sick,
It's strange that we laugh,
I mean, we're not thick.
Still, it's really bad,
And everyone's mad!
They're school dinners
You know!
They're as bad as
Raw dough!
So it really is strange
That we laugh!

Emily Hertzell (10)
Ramsbury Primary School, Marlborough

Smarties

Finally it's in my hand,
Smiling up at me,
Craftily waving its wand,
It's in my mouth,
To die for!

My taste buds are buzzing,
I'm chewing now,
Chocolate bubbling,
Swallowing it zooms down,
My throat is like a spaceship,
I want more . . .
I'm falling apart!

Francesca Barrett (11)
Ramsbury Primary School, Marlborough

I Like to See

I like . . .
A warm comfy bed on a cold winter's night,
The touch of a cold shower after lots of hard exercise,
Sitting down and relaxing to a lovely new book,
Leaving the school boundaries and walking home in the sun,
The sight of my friends playing football at the park.

I don't like . . .
The touch of rain, making me as wet as a whale,
An endless traffic jam when you're late for something important,
The horrid taste of spinach, splashing in my mouth,
But worst of all, being bored and not knowing what to do!

Sam Chapman (11)
Ramsbury Primary School, Marlborough

Six Things Found In An Inquisitor's Cloak

One well-weighted shuriken to decapitate the unbelievers,
A bottle of poison concocted from mashed human brains and eyes,
A bag of fire to incinerate the unworthy,
A hammer filled with a thousand souls, to purge the unclean,
A cross to banish the possessed
And a phial of holy water to cleanse the unrighteous.

Jack Smith (10)
Ramsbury Primary School, Marlborough

Five Things Found On A Dinner Table

One set of sparkling cutlery, shimmering in the candlelight.
Crazy shadows prancing around each other.
Delicious food waiting to be consumed by a delicate character.
Wine, the colour of blood, waits patiently for a man with pure taste.
Finally, fascinating decorations cover the table from head to toe.

David Reynolds (11)
Ramsbury Primary School, Marlborough

A Busy School

S cary teachers bellow at helpless infants,

C areless juniors rampage down corridors,
                kicking bags out of their path.
H ungry dinner ladies jealously watch children
                munching away at their delicious feasts,
O ffended infants begin to cry when their parents
                leave them to enter school,
O bvious coats get trodden on by the raging headmaster,
                holding a naughty child by the scruff of his neck,
L ots of people cheer and play
                as the bell goes for the end of the day.

Leo Dennis (11)
Ramsbury Primary School, Marlborough

Six Things Found In Old Trafford

A memory from a fan when Ryan Giggs scored
                the memorable goal against Arsenal,
A lost Wayne Rooney shirt,
A patch on the pitch where Ronaldo go his studs caught,
A stitch from David Beckham's head,
A well graffitied patch which says
'Go away Malcolm, we are not for sale'.

Gary Hall (11)
Ramsbury Primary School, Marlborough

Five Things Found In A Kangaroo's Pouch

A screaming desert on a hot summer day,
A shimmering sun that looks like a golden globe
                reflecting light on everything around it.
A hump stolen from a camel's back.
The wind guiding a desert storm.
A grain of sand taken from the heat of the sun.

Harry Field (11)
Ramsbury Primary School, Marlborough

Six Things Found In A Fairy's Purse

A shimmering pearl from the Fairy Queen's necklace,
The sparkle from a shooting star.
The shadow of a small child,
All the colours of the rainbow.
A lock of hair from a mermaid,
A spare pair of wings in case of any accidents.

Hattie Clark (11)
Ramsbury Primary School, Marlborough

Six Things Found At The Bottom Of The Queen's Handbag

The old crumpled tissue from last winter that is too dirty
to be thrown away.
The ghastly lid-squashed lipstick that you would need
sunglasses to look at with bare eyes.
The antique wedding ring from a car boot sale that was
given by her fourth husband.
Cracked but clean, the glass slipper from her first ever ball
and the very first one penny coin with her face printed on,
that has a diamond encrusted on the tails side.

Grace Harker (11)
Ramsbury Primary School, Marlborough

Six Things Found In A Mouse's Tail

Some eye drops to keep the eyes sparkling.
A manicure set in case of emergencies.
A wooden shield to protect itself from owls.
Some blusher to keep him looking perky.
A *very* fine comb to brush his whiskers.
Some perfume for those sewer rats.

Lizzie Wilson (10)
Ramsbury Primary School, Marlborough

An Assembly

Terrible teachers go on and on,
Hoping some day their dreams will come true,
Maybe the children will listen to you.

Stupid children at the back,
Natter away about a football match
And of course Trescothic's winning catch.

Innocent infants at the front,
Answer *his* ridiculous requests,
Which are to do with their stupid up and coming tests!

The teacher stressed about the recent actions,
Of a bully's punch,
Which ruined the teacher's lunch,
Stared in annoyance!

Daniel Jones (10)
Ramsbury Primary School, Marlborough

Five Things Found In A Wolf's Fur

A red essence of blood from its last prey,
A shivering howl at the dawn of the day.
A cold wind stolen, never to blow again,
A steaming stench swirling away,
Two pairs of claws to rip its prey.

Harry Swain (11)
Ramsbury Primary School, Marlborough

Five Things Found At The Bottom Of The Sea

A shipwreck that's never been discovered,
A treasure chest full of expensive jewels,
An octopus with ten legs!
An enchanted kingdom full of mermaids, combing their golden hair.
An evil serpent ready to turn you into her slave . . .

Rebecca Court (10)
Ramsbury Primary School, Marlborough

A Day Of School

Ten to nine the bell rings,
A quiet line no one dares to sing,
Straight inside, time for some math,
Oh god, it's really naff.
Now it's time for a break,
Children whizz out like a snake,
Girls start singing skipping rhymes,
Up the climbing frame they climb.
Come back in, it's time for art,
Teachers acting real smart,
Everyone rushes out for lunch,
Their money was replaced with a punch!
Out to play once again,
Everyone puts down their pens,
In again time for PE,
Today we have rounders, hooray, yippee!
All the children smile with glee,
Finally it's ten-past three.

Archie Bhatt-Monro (11)
Ramsbury Primary School, Marlborough

Five Things Found On A Goblin's Bed

A sack full of nightmares ready to be planted
in an innocent child's head,
A giant hammer for smashing into
people's houses,
A twelve-bore shotgun ready to kill
guilty girls,
An old sack for catching tooth fairies,
A cage which had children inside,
The Queen's Crown Jewels resting on
a pillow.

Harry Fisher (11)
Ramsbury Primary School, Marlborough

School Dinners

Crinkled carrots,
Mouldy meatballs,
Sloppy sweetcorn,
Paper plates,
Messy mash,
Rock-hard radish,
Mushy meat,
Smelly steak,
Terrible tomatoes
Cold crème fraiche,
Hard ham
And crunchy chicken.
All in all, school dinners,
Are icky mush
And gooey slush!

Jacob Clay (10)
Ramsbury Primary School, Marlborough

Molly

I have a cat called Molly
And she is very jolly.
When she goes out to play
She likes to run around all day.

She sits in her basket
As sweet as can be,
Hopefully she doesn't have a flea.

She chases birds and mice,
But I still think she is nice.
She sits and plays in the sun,
She's my number one.

Katie Eastman (9)
St Benedict's RC School, Midsomer Norton

Slowly

Slowly it slimes across the ground,
Slowly it goes without a sound,
Slowly it goes, leaving tracks behind it,
Slowly it decides to try and sit.

Slowly it goes,
Slowly, even without toes,
Slowly it goes across the road,
Slowly with a heavy load . . .

Jamilla Griffin (9)
St Benedict's RC School, Midsomer Norton

Slowly

Slowly the tree grows after all the heavy snows.
Slowly all the life will flow.
Slowly back come all the birds,
Slowly their eggs begin to stir.
Slowly bees make their honey,
Slowly it starts to look quite funny.
Slowly like the gentle gush,
Slowly the birds leave in a rush.

Haiden Albrow (9)
St Benedict's RC School, Midsomer Norton

Summer The Cat

Summer the cat,
Likes a nap,
In a hat,
Wearing a cap,
With her toy rat,
On my lap.

Ellie Gilkerson (9)
St Benedict's RC School, Midsomer Norton

The Moon

The moon is bright,
Just like a candle's light,
Wake up soon,
By the light of the moon.
The moon is grace,
Stored in a tiny place.

The morning is near,
Little children never fear,
The cat perching on the wall,
Did you hear the cock call?
I did so hear,
I was standing on the pier.

Morning is coming,
The birds are humming,
The children are stirring,
The mysteries are occurring.
So goodbye to the moon,
I will be seeing you soon!

Hannah Silkstone (9)
St Benedict's RC School, Midsomer Norton

Slowly

Slowly the water goes down the stream,
Slowly it washes it clean.

Slowly the bird goes tu-whit, tu-whoo,
Slowly his wife knows he's true.

Slowly as the sun sets,
Slowly the fishermen pick up their nets.

Slowly come back all the flowers,
Slowly the bees give back all their powers.

Slowly come back all the trees,
Slowly they attract all the bees.

Samantha Mitchell (9)
St Benedict's RC School, Midsomer Norton

Summer Days

Why is it that the hot summer days,
Seem to change your mood and ways?
As we wave winter goodbye,
We always seem to smile and sigh.
Looking forward to the sun and breeze,
Instead of winter's gloomy freeze.
Looking forward to playing outside,
Instead of sitting bored inside.
Summer brings fun, laughter and cheers,
While winter brings out our coldness and fears.
I love summer's happiness and warm days,
That seem to change my mood and ways.

Emily Moon (8)
St Benedict's RC School, Midsomer Norton

Horse Racing

Flashing, dashing on the horse,
Jumping stiles, staying on course.
Trotting onwards through the leaves,
Going onwards through the trees.

Make sure your saddle is on fast,
You never know it might make you last.
Walking onwards till your horse starts feeling frisky,
Breaking into canter then gallop!

Lonneke Kertzman (9)
St Benedict's RC School, Midsomer Norton

Football

Football can be boring
And sometimes can be fun,
I like it when we're scoring
And when my team has won.

Gavin Vincent S Phillips (9)
St Benedict's RC School, Midsomer Norton

The Night Bus

There once was a night bus that travelled by water,
No one knew why it needed a porter.

Were the people on the bus alive?
Well one thing is sure no one could drive.

There were screams and shouts
But no lager louts on the night bus that travelled by water.

Tom Meddings (9)
St Benedict's RC School, Midsomer Norton

Snowy Days

Watch the clouds full of snow
All the flowers will not grow.
In the night our world shall freeze,
The icicles blow in the breeze.
Just staying inside is no fun,
Not like the warm days in the sun.
Outside is bitterly cold,
'Wrap up warm,' that's what I was told!

Verity Rose Hallett (9)
St Benedict's RC School, Midsomer Norton

My Brother

My brother is a mate,
We go to a summer fete.
My dad says if my brother is a pain,
He won't be going to Spain.
I'm glad my brother is great,
Because I wouldn't have such a mate,
Soon he'll be able to jump the garden gate!

Katie Fletcher (9)
St Benedict's RC School, Midsomer Norton

My Football Boots Poem

F lying mud
O n the pitch
O utside playing
T rampling feet
B lowing whistles
A fantastic game
L aughing people
L oving the day

B ottle of Coke
O n the way home
O nce everything has ended
T ravelling fans with an ice cone
S eventeen-nil to City!

Connor Riddle (8)
St Benedict's RC School, Midsomer Norton

Horses

Horses like to walk on their owner's side,
Sometimes they like walking in a land big and wide,
They eat a yellow, straight and bendy straw called hay,
And all the things we usually say,
They understand which they obey.
Also they don't like someone in their way!
In case you haven't noticed they don't all have the same colour
But they have the same taste of flavour.
Horses are very sweet, they gallop like a dog chasing a cat,
And have you ever seen them wearing a hat?
They look smart and gentle,
But sometimes they go mental.

Kris-Mae Dela Isla (9)
St Benedict's RC School, Midsomer Norton

She Was

They were one, as their souls had been welded together in
                              a passionate flame of love.
She was his day and night, his sunrise and sunset.
She was his light, with her he could see all of that which
              lay before him, whether it was glorious or sorrowful.
To him she was his lantern, filled with an internal light
                              of love, hope and rejoice.
He was a great bird gliding through the clear sky,
For she was the graceful wind beneath his swift wings.

But then she was gone.

And so, he was a half once more, as his passionate seal
                              with her melted away.
Neither his sunrise nor sunset came, as his day and night
                              ceased to come.
His moon collapsed, down, down into the deep icy pit of sorrow
And his stars wept as they fled into the darkness of his broken heart.
He was blind to the fate that lay before him.
The rejoice and love in his lantern went out and he was lost in his
                              shattered heart's darkness.
Without her as the graceful wind, he could fly no more . . .

William Hunt (11)
St Benedict's RC School, Midsomer Norton

Me And My Motorbike

My motorbike is yellow and red,
I have to wear a helmet on my head.
When I approach the beginning card,
I need to ensure it won't be too hard.
So when I come to a steep hill,
I have to make sure I keep very still.
Just in case I fall down,
I might get muddy and brown.
Here I am on my last bend,
I rode really well and that's the end.

Charlie Frost (9)
St Benedict's RC School, Midsomer Norton

The Love Of Chocolate

Chocolate, chocolate, chocolate,
Such a nice thing to say,
But it's better in your tummy,
Because you gobble it all away.

Dairy Milk or caramel,
Dark or white,
When you're on a sleepover,
You gobble it all night.

See there're different types of chocolate,
There's the Aero with bubbles,
But don't eat too much,
Because you never know when you might get in trouble.

So don't eat too much,
At the most, two bars a day,
That is still cool,
Come on everyone shout,
'Chocolate! Hooray!'

Radika McCarthy-Singh (10)
St Benedict's RC School, Midsomer Norton

Winter

When winter comes
It becomes so cold.
I am glad I am young
And not too old
Because I will miss out on all the fun
When I am old and not so young.
All day long I play and freeze
As the wind blows through the trees.
The snow falls silently as I go home
And leave my friend all alone.

Westly Frood (9)
St Benedict's RC School, Midsomer Norton

Forest At Night

Forest creaking
Forest speaking
Forest cracking
Forest howling.

Trees rustling
Trees weeping
Trees whispering
Trees sleeping.

Animals creeping
Animals hooting
Animals squeaking
Animals swooping.

Run! Run! *Argh!*

Toby Frayling (9)
St Benedict's RC School, Midsomer Norton

What Am I? Kennings

No legger
Bird eater
Egg layer
Egg eater
Skin shedder
Back boner
Venom fanger
Rat eater
Fork tonguer
Killer biter
Whole swallower.
What am I?

A snake.

Olan Kenny (8)
St Bernard's School, Bristol

What Am I? Kennings

Twitch twitcher
Slip slider
Great runner
Ear flopper
Chase chaser
Rough licker
Four legger
Fur flicker
Tree scratcher
Night walker
Lazy sleeper
Mice chaser.
What am I?

A doggy.

Ornella Navari (9)
St Bernard's School, Bristol

What Am I? Kennings

Body smaller
Tear maker
Cute facer
Small finger
Hard worker
Maybe pinker
Loud crier
Soft skinner
Fast crawler
Thumb sucker
What am I?

A baby.

Krystie-Annah Hooper (9)
St Bernard's School, Bristol

What Am I? Kennings

Meat eater
Night Howler
Fast runner
Teeth razor
Full moon changer
What am I?

A werewolf.

Lewis Barker-Muzzell (9)
St Bernard's School, Bristol

What Am I? Kennings

Old timer
Midnight banger
Three twitcher
Tall stander
Fast timer.
What am I?

A grandfather clock.

Ashley Harrison (8)
St Bernard's School, Bristol

What Am I? Kennings

Oxygen giver,
Food maker,
Soil lover,
Water needer,
Sun seeker
What am I?

A flower.

Ella Calland (8)
St Bernard's School, Bristol

What Am I? Kennings

Good hearer
Back archer
Tree scratcher
Sleep stander
Paw licker
Four legger
Night viewer
What am I?

A cat.

Rosie Shaughnessy (9)
St Bernard's School, Bristol

What Am I? Kennings

Carrot muncher,
Hop runner,
Great slider,
Funny hider.
What am I?

A rabbit.

Tom Jewell (9)
St Bernard's School, Bristol

What Am I? Kennings

Many little, red legs,
Slow mover,
Grey and grumpy,
Small legs,
100 legger!
What am I?

A centipede.

Liam Hawkins (9)
St Bernard's School, Bristol

What Am I? Kennings

Sharp clawer
Long whiskers
Hair shedder
Sofa scratcher
Eye starer
Fur licker
Mice chaser
What am I?

A cat.

Molly Phillips (9)
St Bernard's School, Bristol

What Am I? Kennings

Good fella
Food eater
Grass scratcher
Back scratcher
Hard fella
What am I?

A dog.

Kyle Nolan (9)
St Bernard's School, Bristol

Hate

Hate is black like a vampire's cape
It feels like no one likes me
It smells like red-hot chilli
It tastes like burnt lamb
It sounds like a big, bad headache
It reminds me of all the arguments in my life.

Helen Hulbert (10)
Sambourne Primary School, Warminster

Thetis' Poem

Her necklace, so gold and charming
As she desperately tries to earn the man
She deserves for her three children
Tempted to watch their mother
Get her husband back.

She would jump into the biggest
And hottest volcano, just to save
Her children from absolutely anything.

She is richer than any other lady on Earth
She's wearing the richest blue
Compared to any other person on Earth.
One of her children is wearing
A knight's armour
And he is holding the most precious spear
As she holds the other child of hers
Holding some very special jewellery.
Their mother waits for the man she loves.

Rhys Jones (10)
Sambourne Primary School, Warminster

The Playground

I'm always in the breezy playground
As I am going down the slide,
The wind goes through me,
Like a ghost rushing past me,
By my side.
I'm on the monkey bars with sand in my hand
I fall and hit the ground,
And nobody makes a sound.

Brandon South (10)
Sambourne Primary School, Warminster

Sea Queen

The exploding volcano disturbed the calm, misty sky
And the sea hissed, 'Till death do us die' and
The sea hissed, 'Till death do us die.'
As the moon grew near
Her heart filled with fear
Because she knew she was going to die,
To die - she knew she was going to die.

Her son begged her, 'Please, please do not leave,
Leave us here alone.
I love you so,
So much you know.'
As she dived back into the sea, the sea,
As she dived back into the sea.
As she dived back into the sea.
Our mother we know she loved us so
But she believed in the sea, the sea,
The sea - but she believed in the sea.

Charlotte McDermott (11)
Sambourne Primary School, Warminster

Thetis' Poem

Hair like a black horse leaving a stable.
Blowing through like clouds taking over,
Over the night sky.

Jewels shining from the moon's great gleam.
Like the sun shining on a burning piece of metal.

Clothes as bright as a brand new scarf.
Shirt as silky as a sheep's comfy wool.
Blue trousers as blue as a dark, deep sea.

Jonathan Skinner (11)
Sambourne Primary School, Warminster

Supersonic Sweets

Mint Imperials taste strong
and sound like marbles when you drop them
and they glisten in the sunlight.

Jelly beans and sticky toffees
get stuck between your teeth,
they are so smooth and they taste so sweet.

Jelly Tots and fizzy cola bottles
covered with sugar,
that shines in the daylight.

Irish cream and toffee Aero
that bubbles in your mouth
and tastes so indulgent.

Chewitts that taste very sour
and make you scrunch up your face
are to my liking.

Oliver Nash   (10)
Sambourne Primary School, Warminster

About A Dog

B arking with excitement when I come home
E veryone loves her
S he loves to run in the field
T ickling my face with her big wet tongue

F unny, makes me laugh
R uns through the house
I n and out and has fun
E very day Tara plays in the garden.
N o dog is as good,
D ogs are good friends.

Ryan Hudd   (10)
Sambourne Primary School, Warminster

In The Playground

In the playground every day
Is where I like to run and play.

Laughing and joking with my friends
In the playground, the fun never ends.

Bouncy balls and goalies' nets
Tennis rackets that come in sets.

Making up a silly dance
'Truth or Dare,' I'll take my chance.

But there it goes, the nasty bell
It must be under some kind of spell.

Never mind there's always tomorrow
With 'Truth or Dare' and balls to borrow.

Sophie Skinner (10)
Sambourne Primary School, Warminster

Thetis, The Widow And The Sea Queen

Thetis is a mermaid.
Her hair,
Her hair is like the mane on a lion,
Dark brown and spiky.
Her robe,
Her deep blue, sapphire robe.
Her blouse,
Her emerald, sea-green blouse.
Her children,
Her beautiful, well-loved children.
Her husband,
Her dead husband.

Bethany Usher (10)
Sambourne Primary School, Warminster

Highbury

H ighbury
I ntend to be a
G reat football team
H eroic
B all-stopper, Jason Mundy saved
U nder 10s
R ampaging like a
Y oung keeper should.

A rsenal
R ule
S aints are
E asy to beat
N ewcastle
A re
L osers!

Jamie Denton (10)
Sambourne Primary School, Warminster

Dinosaur

D inosaurs
I nteresting
N obody can stop
O ur
S trong
A mphibious
U seful
R eptiles.

Michael Gemine (10)
Sambourne Primary School, Warminster

Cheetahs

Woodland racing
antelope chasing.

Tree beating
antelope eating.

Meat biting
antelope sneaking.

Wind bracing
antelope breaking.

Darkness rising
antelope tiring.

Sun rising
antelope dying.

Stephen Mathews (10)
Sambourne Primary School, Warminster

Playground

P layground
L ike
A playful
Y oung
G orilla
R unning
O ut of a
U nnecessarily
N oisy
D ugout.

Sam Clift (10)
Sambourne Primary School, Warminster

Super Star Wars

S uper Jedi powers
T riple flips in the air
A mazing Yoda, old and green
R acing Obi Wan

W indu fighting for his life
A fantastic master Jedi Qui-gon Jinn
R aging Anakin turning to the dark side
S uperb Star Wars; like it or lump it!

Rhiannan Player (10)
Sambourne Primary School, Warminster

Star Wars

Star War S
Shining ligh T sabres
Evil, b A d guys
Like Da R th Vader

Anakin Sky W alker
A nd good guys like
Luke Skywalke R and
Jar Jar Bink S.

Mark Dennis Burton (10)
Sambourne Primary School, Warminster

Bobbling Bubbles

B obbling bubbles gliding across the country fields.
U p, up and away, they go into the fine, blue sky.
B ubbles, bubbles,
B ig, clear bubbles flying by the trees, the houses and children
L unging from wall to wall.
E ventually they reach the ground and suddenly . . .

Pop! They're gone.

Katy Ford (10)
Sambourne Primary School, Warminster

The Queen Of The Sea

Hair like a holly bush surrounding a princess' tower
Her clothes as shiny as the bright morning sun
Jewels as delicate as a nest of bird eggs,
Robes of satin-blue dressed all over
As bright as a sapphire ring
Gleaming in the burning hot sun.

As she returns to her faithful locket
After so many years of thinking of the past
As slowly as she can, she opens it
And remembers the past
And in her mind, she truly thought
Her beloved husband was with her
Forever.

Jade Pinnell (10)
Sambourne Primary School, Warminster

The Widow

The locket in her hand, her husband's locket.
Its necklace of pearls attached by a chain.
The picture inside of her great beloved.
Taken from her by the harsh, cruel sea.

She longs for a husband, to help her, to guide her.
To raise her children with love, care and friendship.
Her children are everything to her; they are the stars to her.
They are the ones who guide her through life.

The thorns on her head mark her authority,
The power to share with her husband.
She owns the finest jewels, jewels of the finest quality.

Ben Jeanes (10)
Sambourne Primary School, Warminster

The Sea Queen

Hair like a thorn bush
Surrounding Rapunzel's tower.
Robes as blue as a sapphire
To reveal a symbol of power.

A blouse which has a pattern
To expose her husband's love.
A locket's pearls, just as white
As an exquisite dove.

George Hartnell (11)
Sambourne Primary School, Warminster

What Am I?

I am a grey hunter,
I live in Longleat or in the wild,
I was born in a den,
Under a tree.
I have lots of relations,
One is the dog,
Another, the fox,
So *what am I?*

Clue: Does a river *flow* backwards?

Elizabeth Johnston (10)
Sambourne Primary School, Warminster

Sadness

Sadness, the colour of baby-blue, like the colour of the sky.
Sadness sounds like a fist hitting me in the face.
Sadness tastes like a teardrop in your mouth.
Sadness smells like a drop of blood out of my mouth.
Sadness reminds me of a black eye.
Sadness feels like I want to fall to the ground.

Ben Phelps (10)
Sambourne Primary School, Warminster

The Sea Queen

A thorn bush as her hair
To show how much she cares
For her pair of boys; a pair.

Her shift,
Her blue satin shift.
The shift is a navy blue
That glistens in the morning sun.

The locket in her hand,
Her husband's locket.
Its necklace of pearls,
Attached by a chain,
It lives in her pocket.
The picture inside, of her dearest, beloved,
Taken from her by the cruel, harsh sea.

Thomas Redding (11)
Sambourne Primary School, Warminster

The Sea Queen

Thetis the Sea Queen,
Queen of all the sea,
Wearing the finest silk,
Blue, gold and cream,
Hair entwined with the finest pearls,
Devil-red coral,
Lush, grass-green weed,
Intermingled with chocolate-brown curls,
Dazzling jewels show her power,
As they glisten through the sun-stricken,
                    crystal clear, turquoise sea,
Swimming above the golden yellow sand.

Kirsty Wheeler (11)
Sambourne Primary School, Warminster

The Sea Queen

She is fine,
She is pretty,
To lose her beauty,
Such a pity.

She loves her children,
She loves her clothes,
And in this picture,
She strikes a pose.

Advertising herself to the world,
If she wasn't so desperate,
She wouldn't buy a husband.

She is fine,
She is pretty,
To lose her beauty,
Such a pity.

Hannah Collett (10)
Sambourne Primary School, Warminster

Sea Queen

Blue silken robes
Like a waterfall gushing.
Warm, pure love
Like hot lava rushing.

Shining silver jewels
Cradled within her hands
Strength and power shown
But the way she stands.

Her inside feelings
Are as black as coal
Her broken heart
Empties her soul.

Nicola Mousley (11)
Sambourne Primary School, Warminster

The Sea Queen

Her robe is as silky as
The navy-blue sky.

Her hair is as black as a
Thunderstorm going on for days.

Her locket is as shiny as a golden egg,
With the smile of her husband.

Her blouse is as gold
As a necklace.

As their mum is loving,
She will die for her children.

Shaun Marlow (11)
Sambourne Primary School, Warminster

The Wind

As I tiptoe through the air
Rustling the leaves on trees
Weaving in and out of little girls' hair
A cool and gentle breeze.

But I assure you
When I'm angry
Stay well clear
For I will punch and attack
With all my mighty power
I will look at you and glower
For I am a bully
And I'll roar in the face of my foe.

Now I am calm again
And I'm feeling so much better
There's no reason to be scared
Suddenly sleepiness has overcome me
I will rest until another day.

Jorden Kenyon & Paige Williams (11)
Shirehampton Junior School, Bristol

My Uncle Sam Is . . .

As weird as the weather
As fat as a rock
As *tall* as a giant
As hairy as a sock.

As black as a goth
As dull as a *loss!*
As dumb as a dog
As fashionable as Kate Moss.

As smelly as the sewers
As fast as lightning
As *bald* as an *egg*
And he is always *crying!*

Aaron Harvey & Luke Carey (9)
Shirehampton Junior School, Bristol

Summer's Day

Summer's day is on its way
It's just before autumn day.

In summer we bathe in the sun
And eat lots of yummy buns.

Don't forget Christmas is in a while
And so let's see the River Nile.

So let's eat cakes
Then buy shakes.

Let our friends come round
And make lots of sounds.

Summer's day is on its way
It's just before autumn's day.

Yacine Nouq, Joe Carter & Joe Golder
Shirehampton Junior School, Bristol

My Dog Spot

I have a white dog
whose name is Spot.
Well he's sometimes white
but sometimes not.
Whether he's white
or whether he's not,
he's still the greatest
dog called Spot.

He likes a bone
and likes a ball,
but he doesn't care
for a cat at all.
He waggles his tail
and he knows what's what.
So I'm glad to say that he's my dog,
my dog Spot.

Tara Louise Dixon (10)
Shirehampton Junior School, Bristol

The Daft Cousin

I've got a very daft cousin
That's as daft as a clown
She's as fat as a doughnut
And her hair is very brown.

She's as loud as a whoopee cushion
As jazzy as a DJ
As mean as a witch
And she likes to wear her PJs.

She's as stretchy as an elastic band
She's as dumb as a brick wall
She's as rocking as a band
She likes to play football!

Katie Ackerman, Laura Jones & Amy West (9)
Shirehampton Junior School, Bristol

What's Lurking In Your Room?

In *my* room I've got:
10 ferocious lions behind my bedroom door
9 eye-popping spiders underneath the sheets
(don't show them to Mum)
8 garish geckos sticking to the ceiling
7 spine-shuddering boas underneath the floorboards
6 jaw-dropping polar bears lurking in the wardrobe
5 jaw-snapping crocodiles in my underpants' drawer
4 extraordinary elephants sleeping in my desk
3 fascinating flying squirrels inside the antique chest
2 long lanky giraffes lurking inside the linen bin
1 greedy sausage dog squashed inside my violin case.

I've shown you what's in my room, what's in yours?

Danielle Hodges (9)
Shirehampton Junior School, Bristol

Animal Parades

A nimals parading
N aughty monkeys jumping around
 I t's the animal parade
M others watching for their young
A nimal parade
L ions leading as they like.

P artridges fly in the sky
A nimals are loving it because it's animal parade
R oosters cock-a-doodle-doo all day long
A nimal parade
D ingos resting with other animals
E veryone's joining in the animal parade!

Kimberley Chapman (11)
Shrewton Primary School, Salisbury

Messenger Poem

You pass twinkling lights as you go,
Flying swiftly to and fro.
You see fairies dancing,
All creatures prancing.
Your golden wings carry you on,
Through the sky you're having fun.
You have come to your victory,
To put people out of misery.
Your wings start to slow down,
As you reach the firm ground.
They ask you for a reply,
And you say with all hopes high,
'We are going to be alright
Through the day and the whole night.'
You are safe now forever . . .

Emma Palmer (11)
Shrewton Primary School, Salisbury

Egypt

When I worked day and night, day and night
To build a pyramid for the mighty man, man,
I always cried in pain building, building.
When I carried blocks of stone I thought my life had ended, ended.
Then one day my dream came true, a pyramid had been
                                        finished, finished,
All of a sudden my pharaoh's life had ended sadly, sadly.
We embalmed the pharaoh, how sad it was, I could not watch, watch,
Then one day my life had ended, I guess my family was so sad, sad.
I hope my son took on my job and had a happy life, and had a
                                        happy life.

Jane Brown (11)
Shrewton Primary School, Salisbury

I Am Free

One rampage through the house and out,
We went to a truck,
To the train station we were sent,
Put in a cattle carriage and taken away.

Two days of near suffocation,
We were taken out and sorted slowly,
Children and elders were taken away
To the gas chamber, some say,
Twelve everlasting years I spent there,
Working, hurting,
I found some trust in a man
Who helped me on my way,
A confined space no more,
The vast acres were mine,
I was free.

On my way I slowly went
To Salonica then Denmark.

Struggling on my slow way,
I was there at Salonica,
I stayed there a couple of nights, then on my way I went,
Clean and fresh up the hill,
I trudged up and up,
Northwards, northwards, I must go and meet Denmark,
But now I am *free!*

Ellie Selby (11)
Shrewton Primary School, Salisbury

Wild Wee Willie

Wee Willie Winkie, driving us bananas
Upstairs and downstairs in his pink pyjamas
Rap and disco, pop and rock
Turn that flaming music off,
It's past *twelve o'clock!*

Joe Johns (10)
Shrewton Primary School, Salisbury

The Bear Who Cried To Go Home

I've been here for some months now
Dancing for this man
I'm really tired and homesick
Just to fill his can

Everyone sees me dancing
This really isn't me
I'm used to hunting in forests
And searching rivers for my tea

I like to hear the children laugh
But they do not understand
If they did not visit me
I would go home to my native land

You could always come and see me there
But view me from afar
Just like a game safari
Instead of behind bars, you would see me from a car.

You would not see me dancing
Just me being a bear
If you would still like to visit me
I would love to see you there.

Lauren Harwood (10)
Shrewton Primary School, Salisbury

Laughter

Laughter is as bright a yellow as the morning sun.
It tastes like the sweet apples of Heaven.
It sounds like the gentle fluttering of fairy wings.
It looks like a smile on the face of Faith herself.
It smells like the warm smell of toast in the morning.
It feels as warm and fluffy as a little bunny rabbit.
Laughter reminds me of all things soft and cuddly.

Nicole Esdaile (10)
Sutton Veny CE Primary School, Warminster

Fear

Fear is black like the darkest plum,
It smells like a fire spreading through a building,
It tastes like a bruised banana,
It feels like a ball of spikes that never stops rolling after you,
It looks like a blob that changes into your worst nightmares,
It sounds like a person screaming as they fall down an empty shaft.
Fear reminds me of a black dog snarling as you try to get past.

Fear!

Max Betteridge (11)
Sutton Veny CE Primary School, Warminster

Darkness

Darkness is black like the sky at midnight.
Darkness looks like a bottomless pit with skeletons rotting
at the bottom.
Darkness feels like an earthquake ripping through your heart.
Darkness tastes like punch made of blood.
Darkness sounds like a cave with a never-ending echo.
Darkness smells like a gloomy prison.
Darkness reminds me of death.

Alexander Mitchell (11)
Sutton Veny CE Primary School, Warminster

Jealousy

Jealousy is red like the anger that runs through your veins.
Jealousy looks like fresh blood squeezed out of a wolf.
Jealousy feels like a volcano melting your soul.
Jealousy tastes like blood dripping on raw meat.
Jealousy smells like rotting fish covered in blood.
Jealousy sounds like blood dripping off the top of a cave.
Jealousy reminds me of my friends showing off.

Jeremy Smith (11)
Sutton Veny CE Primary School, Warminster

Hate

Hate is black like a dark, bottomless pit.
Hate sounds like a giant's step thundering in your ear.
Hate tastes bitter like cold coffee and burning chillies
                                    scorching your insides.
Hate feels like a dagger stabbing through your heart
                                    and wiping out your soul.
Hate smells like a rotten fish from the night before.
Hate looks like a red, burning hole, grabbing you and
                                    pulling you down, further in.
Hate reminds me of people hurting and dying all around.

Bianca Wolkenstein (11)
Sutton Veny CE Primary School, Warminster

Summer

Summer is golden like the shimmering sun that's high in the sky
Summer tastes like melting ice cream dripping down to the floor
Summer smells like flowers spreading their scents everywhere
Summer sounds like birds fluttering through the midday sky
Summer looks like a sweet shop bursting with colours
Summer feels like seaside fun filling your heart with joy
Summer reminds me of children playing games in the fresh,
                                    dewy grass.

Rebecca Young (10)
Sutton Veny CE Primary School, Warminster

Darkness

Darkness is black like a witch's cat riding on a witch's broom
                                    at midnight.
It looks like a pirate's flag blowing in the wind.
It tastes like death that murders your soul.
It smells like a pirate's breath that burns your nose.
It sounds like pure emptiness filling an empty room.
It reminds me of my aunt's funeral.

Benjamin Dews (10)
Sutton Veny CE Primary School, Warminster

Summer

Summer is a mixture of colours, blue, yellow, green and orange.
For blue, the sky.
For yellow, the sun.
For green, the hills.
For orange, the faraway fields.

Summer smells like flowers and roses mixed together.
Summer looks like a rainbow, turquoise sea smashing against it.
Summer tastes like fresh fruit with strawberries and pineapple.
Summer reminds me of acres of hills and fields full of flowers.
And a place where the sun shines straight at you.

Lee Cooper (11)
Sutton Veny CE Primary School, Warminster

Envy

Envy is red like a tomato that's been thrown up at the stage,
Envy smells like a foul stinking rotten egg.
Envy tastes like a lemon that's bitter when it touches a taste bud in
your mouth.
Envy looks like a burnt, black piece of toast.
Envy sounds like crushed egg being smashed to pieces.
Envy feels like tied shoelaces inside your stomach.
Envy reminds me of my friends boasting.

Becky Prior (11)
Sutton Veny CE Primary School, Warminster

Envy

Envy is green like the leaves in the jungle.
It tastes bitter like lemon and lime, freshly squeezed into a glass.
It smells like freshly made manure in a farmyard.
It looks ugly like a wart on your knee.
It sounds like echoing footsteps walking away.
It feels like rotten apples being thrown at you.
It reminds me of my friends showing off in front of me.

Fergus Frank (10)
Sutton Veny CE Primary School, Warminster

Darkness

Darkness is black, like the black panther's fur.
It sounds like your breath, bouncing back from the nothingness.
It tastes like a lemon, stinging your tongue.
It looks like the gaping jaws of a tiger stretching its throat.
It smells like a cellar, abandoned for years.
It feels like the air, dark and damp.
Darkness reminds me of being lonely for hours.
    Darkness.

Henry John (10)
Sutton Veny CE Primary School, Warminster

Fear

Fear is like bloodshed from a battle.
It looks dead like a lifeless soul lying in a coffin.
It feels like your heart pounding when you open a door
                      to see what's inside.
It sounds like the whistling of the wind at midnight.
It smells like a dead corpse in the heat.
It tastes like sweat trickling down your cheek.
It reminds me of a twisting, turning roller coaster.

Cameron Halkett (11)
Sutton Veny CE Primary School, Warminster

Silence

Silence is white like the running core of the sun,
Silence smells like fresh air on a dewy morning,
Silence sounds like the peaceful afterlife,
Silence tastes like fresh milk mixed with pepper,
Silence feels like the sharp pain of being rejected,
Silence looks like a bright white light,
Silence reminds me of death.

Seth Roberts (10)
Sutton Veny CE Primary School, Warminster

Happiness

Happiness is bright like the summer sun on the hottest day of the year.
Happiness feels like the warmth of your mother's arms around you
in a birthday hug.
Happiness tastes like a warm cookie that has just come out of a
hot oven.
Happiness smells like a sweet flower, bright in the sunrise.
Happiness looks like a smile that never fades.
Happiness sounds like the sweet twitter of a happy bird's song.
Happiness reminds me of fun and joyful games with my best friends.

Jennifer Irons (10)
Sutton Veny CE Primary School, Warminster

Happiness

Happiness is pink like a newly-grown rosebud.
Happiness smells like a chocolate shop as you walk by.
Happiness sounds like the twittering birds in the morning.
Happiness feels like a hug from your best friend as you make up.
Happiness tastes like ripe strawberries and snow-white cream.
Happiness looks like a sick person being well again.
Happiness reminds me of the love all my family and friends give me.

Happiness.

Lauren McComish (10)
Sutton Veny CE Primary School, Warminster

Happiness

Happiness is yellow like the sun smiling.
Happiness sounds like children playing.
Happiness tastes like a hot chocolate cake.
Happiness smells like a good day.
Happiness looks like children playing in the park.
Happiness feels like you have the best news in the world.
Happiness reminds me of being with my family and friends.

Lucy Waters (11)
Sutton Veny CE Primary School, Warminster

Fun

Fun is bright orange like the bright warm sun in the middle of summer.
Fun tastes like sweet, pink candyfloss from the fairground.
Fun feels like a day you never ever want to end.
Fun sounds like birds tweeting and people joyfully laughing.
Fun looks like a circus full of rainbow colours with a blue sky above
on a spring day.
Fun smells like fresh, hot doughnuts cooking in the wind.
Fun reminds me of a day with just me and my friends having a great
day out together.

Fun.

Zöe Fitzgerald (11)
Sutton Veny CE Primary School, Warminster

Laughter

Laughter is pink like a rose.
Laughter sounds like a group of people who have just heard a joke.
Laughter smells like a new, fresh day.
Laughter feels like someone's just told the best joke in the world.
Laughter tastes like chocolate cake.
Laughter looks like a sign of goodness.
Laughter reminds me of friendship.

Katie Lampard (11)
Sutton Veny CE Primary School, Warminster

Hate

Hate is pitch-black, like an endless cavern.
Hate looks like sharp, black spikes.
Hate tastes like blood mixed with vinegar.
Hate smells like bad eggs and sour milk at a wonderful feast.
Hate feels like a black, sticky bog in the middle of the night.
Hate sounds like a sharp cry piercing the midnight air.
Hate reminds me of being left out in a game.

Louis McBride (10)
Sutton Veny CE Primary School, Warminster

Happiness

Happiness is yellow like a sunflower
following the sun across the sky.

Happiness tastes like a marshmallow
when you get a happy feeling inside you.

Happiness smells like melting chocolate
when it drips over the saucepan.

Happiness feels like when you run
your toes through a fluffy rug.

Happiness looks like pink baubles
swaying in the wind.

Happiness sounds like a newborn lamb
calling to its mother.

Happiness reminds me of
hugging my teddy as I fall asleep.

Rosie Hall (11)
Sutton Veny CE Primary School, Warminster

Fear

Fear is black like looking around in a boggy swamp at midnight.
Fear feels like a twisting tornado turning through the centre of
your soul.
Fear tastes like ash, tossing and churning inside your mouth
so that you are unable to swallow.
Fear looks like two warriors fighting for their lives whilst
others are pleading not to be struck down.
Fear sounds like a gunshot powering itself through your
mind that never ceases.
Fear smells like the blood on an honourable soldier's blade.
Fear reminds me of feeling the death of a loved one.

Ben Winter (11)
Sutton Veny CE Primary School, Warminster

Anger

Anger is dark crimson, like the red of blood.
Anger tastes like the sourest lemons and the bitterest blood.
Anger sounds like the high-pitched buzzing of wasps and a deep
pounding drumbeat.
Anger looks like a whirlpool of crimson, dragging you down into its
deep depths.
Anger feels like a sticky, drying pool of fresh blood.
Anger smells like burnt turnips cooked with rotten tomatoes.
Anger reminds me of a cold, dark place, like the inside of a
pile of ashes.

Rebecca Freestone (10)
Sutton Veny CE Primary School, Warminster

Tiddlywinks

In one final bid
the brave, stupid kid
thought Tiddlywinks couldn't cause harm
he tiddled too strong and it went far and long
and set off a burglar alarm!

Ollie Harper-Bill (9)
The Tynings CP School, Bristoll

The Dog Next Door

The dog next door was called Ben.
He used to be a farmer's dog and chase all the hens.
His best mates were Major Bonnie and Pip
When he came in from play he was muddy so he used to slip.
I really love him so much that I would see him again and again.

Emily McCoy (10)
The Tynings CP School, Bristol

If Only I Could Go Back To . . .

If only I could go back to Tudor times
To see the streets filled with grime.

If only I could go back to see the Victorians
To see for myself what's said by historians.

If only I could see the Romans
To go to the Coliseum to see a showman.

If only I could go back through all the ages
If I had a time machine I could flip through time like a book of pages!

George Jefferies (10)
The Tynings CP School, Bristol

As The Sun Goes Down

As the sun goes down,
What can you hear, what can you see?
Squirrels bustling, hustling, rustling,
Owls calling too-wit-too-woo, too-wit-too-woo,
People snoring; snort, snort,
That is what you can hear and see,
As the sun goes down.

Alice Wood (10)
The Tynings CP School, Bristol

My Camp Diary

On the trapeze,
Oh what a breeze,
Abseil the wall,
Hope I don't fall,
Climbing up the climbing wall.

Nic Shore (10)
The Tynings CP School, Bristol

My Cats

I have a cat called Sid who is very ginger,
but, the thing is, he's quite a whinger.
I have a cat called Harry who is grey and white
and he can't put up much of a fight.

But I love my cats so much,
they are the friendliest pets to touch.

I keep the front door open for just one minute
and the cats think, *oh let's get out of here innit*.
Harry is sweet from bottom to top,
But when he goes down the stairs; *bop, bop, bop.*

But I love my cats just the way they are,
Just as long as they don't go really far.

I shout to my cats, 'Wait.'
But then they spill a load of paint!
If other cats were just as nice, I wish, wish, wish
and oh by the way, did I mention I have some fish?

Shaun Flook (10)
The Tynings CP School, Bristol

My Little Fishy

My little fish is as gold as the sun
My little fish is as fast as lightning
My little fish has a tank fit for a king
My little fish has a rest.

My little fish likes his food
My little fish hates our cat
My little fish swims around all day
My little fish is the *best!*

Calum McDonald (10)
The Tynings CP School, Bristol

The New Kid

When I went to school, he was sitting in my place,
With huge antennas and an ugly green face,
I asked it for my chair back, but it said, 'No way,
Because my name is Jack and I'm here to stay.'
I tried to be polite, but he got me really mad,
So I made fun of the fourteen fingers he had.
Then he got really cheesed off, shoved me to the floor
And kicked me so hard I went flying out the door.
I laid there on the cold tiles in so much pain,
It felt as if I'd got six of the best from the cane.
The new kid came striding out and challenged me to a fight,
So I got up and punched him with all my might.
He then turned around and had me in his sights,
So he pulled out his ray gun, then came a flash of light.
I woke up in the hospital, all tucked up in bed,
I looked up to see the alien kid's, big, green head.
But he was surrounded by others of his kind,
So I peered out of the window, only to find,
I wasn't in a hospital; I was on a spaceship
And I'd had a very long trip!

Daniel McCarthy (10)
The Tynings CP School, Bristol

Love You Forever

She came into the classroom like a beautiful dove
as soon as I saw her, my eyes filled with love.
She came and sat down next to me
I almost fainted when she gazed to see.
Even now she's gone
she's still my number one.
Nothing will change that, I'll love her forever
but the time that will be - never.

Rowan James (10)
The Tynings CP School, Bristol

Football Match

I like football, it's the best
I even like playing in my vest
I play on snow, I play on grass
Everyone says I am the best in the class.
Football, football, all the time
But I always make sure the ball is mine
We like to win and get the cup
But when we lose, it's just bad luck.
I go to watch the England team
Being a footballer is my dream
In sun and rain I play the game
But my football kit has stayed the same.
Midfield is my best position
And the referee makes the decisions
At the end of the day I go to cool down
And watch the sun shine all around.

Jacob Wiltshire (10)
The Tynings CP School, Bristol

Cuddly Pets

C ute and cuddly, sometimes the best,
U sually good, but sometimes naughty,
D aft and dumb, make hearts melt,
D evoted and loyal, you can trust,
L oud and squawky maybe suits you,
Y ou have to give them love and care

P ets are the best,
E verybody knows,
T ickly, lovely pets,
S o we all love pets.

Jodie Britton (10)
The Tynings CP School, Bristol

Seasons

When winter comes
It gets very cold
Rain falls and we get wet
Trees and flowers are watered
When it snows, children smile,
A snowman they can build.

Springtime comes,
Flowers start to bloom,
The sun shines down,
On the early morning dew,
The leaves turn green,
The birds begin to sing.

Summer follows spring,
The sun shines bright,
This is the season we all like,
Shorts and T-shirts we all wear,
Sandcastles on the beach,
Children splashing in the sea.

The autumn wind,
Begins to blow,
The leaves down from the trees,
Laid on the ground,
A brown, crisp layer,
Leaves no longer green.

Hope Bowyer (10)
The Tynings CP School, Bristol

The Pet I Want . . .

I want a pet,
I want a pet,
I want a pet and I'll get one, I bet,
One that's very fun,
One that doesn't just laze in the sun.
I want a pet,
I want a pet,
I want a pet that won't get me wet,
One that doesn't growl,
One that doesn't even scowl.
I want a pet,
I want a pet,
I want a pet and I haven't got one yet,
One that isn't very big,
One that hardly ever digs.
I want a pet,
I want a pet,
I want a pet that doesn't ever fret,
One that doesn't bite,
One that I can cuddle all night.
I want a pet,
I want a pet,
I want a pet that doesn't always go to the vet,
One that can be my friend,
Our friendship will never end.
I want a pet,
I want a pet,
I got the one I set out to get.

Eleanor Sheppard (10)
The Tynings CP School, Bristol

My Favourite Things

He's black and white,
So big and bright,
So full of beans,
On my chair he leans,
He's Charlie my dog,
Who sleeps like a log
And is one of my favourite things.

The crayons all new,
Yellow, pink and blue,
I sit on my stool
And use them at school,
My felt tip pack
And my crayon stack,
They're one of my favourite things.

So pink and pretty,
All nice and glittery,
With a pink heart mirror,
To see things clearer,
It has private locks,
My big jewellery box,
It's one of my favourite things.

To make it come true,
To have fun with you,
My family, my friends,
It never ends,
It is my scheme,
My favourite dream,
That's really my favourite thing.

Victoria Wright (10)
The Tynings CP School, Bristol

My Glorious Pets

Rat-a-tat-tat,
That's Ellie and Rose,
Searching and sniffing,
Through their nose,
Where's our lunch?
They're searching around.
At last their lunch,
They have found.

Her barking is near,
Peb's calling my name,
I look to my rear,
She's ready for games,
Her ears upright and alert,
Her tail wagging madly,
I throw her toy, Bert,
That lands on the dirt,
Peb retrieves it gladly.

Whiskers and Patch are waiting,
For their breakfast to arrive,
I rush to feed them, without fainting,
I care about their lives.

Slippery smooth, hissing, spooky,
That's my bro's pet snake,
Forked tongue in and out,
A bit like a garden rake,
Finds his prey, lashes out,
Squeezing, won't let go,
Now it's all in his mouth,
Gulp, swallow, bye-bye foe.

Sam Evans (10)
The Tynings CP School, Bristol

Playtime Panic!

Hooray! Hooray! It's time for play,
let's get moving on our way.

Pick up our coats, rush out the door,
running so fast I fall on the floor.

At last! At last! I'm out in the fresh air,
the wind is blowing against my hair.

Find my friends, I say hi,
'What shall we play?' I say with a sigh.

Let's play football with the boys,
they are making such a noise.

Up goes the hand for the end of play,
walking in, we're on our way.

Working hard for the rest of the day,
can't wait for the next play.

Rebecca Walsh (10)
The Tynings CP School, Bristol

My Friend Arnie

I have a dog whose name is Arnie,
He barks and jumps and sends us barmy!
When food's about he cries and whinges,
Just as if he hasn't been fed for ages.
Our cat, he loves, he licks and cuddles,
His food he eats when no one's watching.
So when you knock on our door when calling,
All you'll hear is my dog barking.
Your feet he'll bite, a nip, a tussle,
But really all he wants is trouble.
He's fun, he's friendly,
He's my friend Arnie.

Lauren Handford (10)
The Tynings CP School, Bristol

The Fight

There once was a boy called Sid,
Who one day flipped his lid,
He got really mad,
He's a really angry lad,
Then came this other kid.

They got into a fight,
Their eyes got really tight,
Sid got punched in the head,
He was nearly knocked dead,
That was the end of the fight.

The very next day,
They woke up in dismay,
They became best friends,
Their friendship to mend,
Their differences had gone away.

Callum Flett (9)
The Tynings CP School, Bristol

Icicles

Mystical colours reach out for you
Into the prisoned icicles, icicles
Rainbow colours jump and dash
Into your eyes, icicles.
The soft peppermint touches,
The icicles art delicately
Ice covers bicycles.

Enchantment of the wind swoops
Icicles rest upon the pine
It's magically mixing all in mind
Which makes my heart divine
Ice is the song I hear
Which makes me want to laugh and cheer.

Alice Nugent (9)
Wanborough Primary School, Swindon

Blazing Fire

The fire's burning
It's spitting flames,
As red as a berry
As bright to his name.
It will sway and swing,
As along with it we sing.

The fire's glowing
As long as it sings,
The guard is its shield
The warmth that it brings.
It crackles and roars like a lion,
The colours of the fire are Hawaiian.

The flames how they dance
And smile with glee
It's like a man on a horse
I wish it was me,
As the fire dies, the flames, still fighting,
The room no glow, all dark, no lighting.

Alice Roberts (10)
Wanborough Primary School, Swindon

Romance Is . . . Haiku

Romance is soppy,
Soppy, disgusting, girly,
Grown-up and kissy.

Romance is girly,
Boys do not like it really,
Hearts and kisses, love.

Romance is grown-up,
Lovely, disgusting, silly,
Pink and red love hearts.

Olivia Tuck (8)
Wanborough Primary School, Swindon

The Theme Park

The ride is a fast athlete running,
But some are slow toddlers crawling,
I wonder where a good ride is,
My map tells me my favourite one,
This one swerves like a dancing queen,
I go so high, I'm not seen.

The ride jogs round his course,
But he comes back and arrives for me,
So I jump on when it comes to stop
And when I'm on, we fly off,
I see the queues as long as rainbows,
It is really fun, but also slow.

Now I'm off I sway like grass in the breeze,
The noise is as loud as a nest of birds,
I scream at the downfall vertical drop,
Hip hip hooray, it's not busy
Earlier it was like a beehive
Really busy, bees doing a jive.

Katie Pullan (10)
Wanborough Primary School, Swindon

Football Tanka

Football is so great
Football can be aggressive
Teams win, lose or draw
It is an exciting game
Football is the world's best sport.

Alex Babington (8)
Wanborough Primary School, Swindon

360 Flame

Its horns dazzle in the light of a diamond
The eyes as blue as a hot spring
As the cursed ring lies between the scales
Its teeth like an army of swords
As its flames dance through the air
Like a tired man, sleeping in his lair.

The scales like a crystal of brown, red and green
A hunter with a mouth of a gun, the hunters will be
Hunted its claws is a chainsaw, it rumbles for food
The feet scrape the ground for earthquakes
A tail like a cloud in danger
Its shape is a black stranger.

Its wings are unleashed on the mountain
And it flies like a jet
The sea of fire
The power of smoke
The stirring of wind
The dragon meat clings.

Daniel Waldron (9)
Wanborough Primary School, Swindon

Gymnastics

Handstands jump off vault
Four gold, one silver medal
On the track training
Cartwheels and flat-backs too
It is my favourite sport.

A competition
Everyone is watching you
You find out your score
Third and second are announced
Finally the winner's named.

Jessica Ridler (9)
Wanborough Primary School, Swindon

The 3 Seasons

I look out the window
And see autumn is breaking
The trees are swaying in the breeze
Like a herd of buzzing bees
The leaves are floating like a feather
The leaves feel as soft as leather.

The snow is falling
It is a glorious sight
The snowflakes are fairies
The church is called Saint Mary's
The children are having fights
With the jumping children with might.

The flowers are growing
Everybody's mowing
The flowers are dancing
Easter is near
So never fear.

Megan Paper (10)
Wanborough Primary School, Swindon

Mythical Creatures Haikus

Witches on broomsticks
Ghosts that go woo in the night
Monsters that go roar.

Vampires that suck blood
Jack Frost with his icy hand
Fairies with big wings.

Elves that are naughty
Goblins that work for evil
Sea serpents that swim.

Olivia Witts (8)
Wanborough Primary School, Swindon

Space

The stars flew in darkness all day long
They hovered sadly alone,
Then all at once they began to fly
Up high above the moon,
They were diamonds flying with their wings
On the Milky Way with friends and other things.

The Milky Way is a colourful thing
With its colours all merged together,
It danced and span like a perfect dancer
All dressed in sky-blue clothes,
The Milky Way twisted and twirled
As it looks down on our wonderful world.

The planets are spaced all around the stars
The moon drips like cream,
The sun spits fire all around
Past Pluto shaped like a ball,
As small it seems; planet Mars,
As off we fly, say bye to the stars.

Jonathon Nicholls (9)
Wanborough Primary School, Swindon

The World

The world is special,
I find it a happy place,
Third planet to the sun,
Important God, to the world,
I live in England, Europe!

Great place here now,
New things come every day,
Things, always changing,
It is a bad and good world
Wars, fights, losing homes here now!

Hannah Mills (9)
Wanborough Primary School, Swindon

The Sun

The sun is a golden coin
The spitting flames spring out like grease in a pan
The sun sizzles and boils like a stove
Its flames twizzle out like a flame thrower
Its fantastic scorching ray
Blasts down on the people and knows the sun has come to stay.

Its red and orange fire soothes the meditating mind
The sun's imprisoned flame rings
Pour out and melt metal into cream
Its fiery, dancing soul is as graceful as a swordfish
Its awesome, powerful starlight blaze
Makes the creamy silver stars look at it in a daze.

It pounces into the sky like a leopard
The sun is a topaz stone in the sky like caramel
The sun glints down upon us like a gem of life
The sun is a drop of juice lost from a jug
The sun will never, ever leave, or let us down
The king of the universe, the jewel of a crown.

Daniel Thomas (10)
Wanborough Primary School, Swindon

Sports

Playing football is the best
Taking their shirts off, showing their vest
Cricket is another sport we all like to do
Shouting, running around, getting sweaty too.

Playing football is the best
Score a goal in the net
Quick gymnastics all over the place
Safety mats down just in case.

Bradley Mitchell (9)
Wanborough Primary School, Swindon

Football

The ball is soaring through the air like an aeroplane.
Jumping when you score a goal
When the game is finished there are sweaty T-shirts
The keeper is saving shots
The crowd are in their lots.

The players are celebrating and jumping
The crowds cheering and shouting
Ref that was a foul, come on!
Wayne Rooney has a super shot
Ronaldo does tricky tricks
And Wes Brown is number 6.

Players are speedy like cars
All they do is kick it
They tackle hard as a rhino
Getting injuries is not good at all
When they score they jump up and down
You hear a lot of sound.

Ben White (10)
Wanborough Primary School, Swindon

The Beach

The golden sand glistens in the sun
Like a bar of gold in a bank.
The sea is a vast ocean,
That shimmers in the sun.
The waves dance and sway,
The beach has come here to stay.

The sand shimmers,
Like a roaring fire.
It glistens and sparkles
Dancing in the slight breeze.
The seaweed tussles with my feet,
I know that the beach has gone to sleep.

Jack Mason (10)
Wanborough Primary School, Swindon

The Forest

The forest trees shoot up like a rocket
With the shoots dancing with the wind
The treetops are lockets
The tree trunks grinned
With the deer standing proud
The birds in a crowd.

The plants twist and twirl
With grace and pace
The flowers are white like a pearl
The stems are hard lace
The roses are like fire
The forest is free of wire.

The hills tower up high
With no houses
The bushes have ties
And also have mouses
The moon has come out
That's how the day is spelt.

Bethany Meaden (10)
Wanborough Primary School, Swindon

The Beach

The sun sparkles on the sea
Palm trees like to dance and sway,
The golden silk lies soft and sound
The water shimmers in the breeze,
Seaweed comes to see me as it sits on my feet
All is calm as the beach sleeps.

The fluffy white clouds stare
As they move away,
The seagull's squawk deafens me
I stand in the water,
It's as cold as ice
The breeze is cooling, all is nice.

Megan Street (10)
Wanborough Primary School, Swindon

The Garden

The garden is a cherished place
The garden is a beautiful scent,
The flowers like to race
I am glad that I went.
The garden is a smile to flowers
And it is full of powers.

The begonia is my wisdom
They are a purple haze,
Ruling all the kingdom
This is Heaven's maze.
The petals are round warts
They shine like purple quartz.

The tulips are red with extreme
They sway with the wind,
Even as beautiful as they seem
But secretly a fiend.
They are a red filled shock
But overall they rock!

Callum Egan   (10)
Wanborough Primary School, Swindon

Snowfall

The snow is falling all around me
The air is freezing cold
The icicles are dancing to and fro
The moon shines on the ice as if it was painting
Snow falls like fire
It goes on through the night, it will never tire.

The snow shadow is a white stranger
Snow is a silver star playing in the moon
Snow falls before it melts
In the morning the snow is cool
Nice and straight
And has no weight.

Oliver Berwick   (10)
Wanborough Primary School, Swindon

The Meadow

The wildflowers sing and dance in the breeze
The meadow comes alive and walks over to me
Trees start to chatter to their neighbours
A blue sky looks down on me
Bunnies jump through the long grass
I come through a gate as hard as brass.

What seems like hundreds of different flowers stare at me
Birds hum tunes to each other like a musical code
A rainbow looks back at me when I see the flowers
Like bugs and creatures talk to each other
I hear a grasshopper and cricket, both make a sound
I can't hear my footsteps when I step on the ground.

The blaze of grass twists and turns
The sun shines when the trees tell it to
All of a sudden the flowers start to dance once more
The badgers whisper and run gracefully
Everything is still, the wind stops blowing
The animals run home all steps flowing.

Christie Batty (10)
Wanborough Primary School, Swindon

Tanka Animals

Chickens go cluck cluck.
Horses chomp while they eat. Yum!
Cows are spotty black.
Cats go yummy with their fish.
Dogs roll around madly mad.

Wolves growl in forests.
Foxes howl in garden's bush.
Mouses go eek eek.
Rabbits go boing, boing, bounce, hop.
Birds tweet, tweet and sing a song.

Lina Kumasaka (7)
Wanborough Primary School, Swindon

Snow Angel

The freeze of an angel
Cold as ice
Pretty blonde hair
Sways in the night
Her white wings
As light as pins.

The deep blue body
Blue like the sea
Eyes like jumping raindrops
Nothing pretty as she
Singing wings
This is what the snow brings.

Slick lips
Ready to sing
Hands like wool
Not a single ring
Hair straight as a line
She has a cloak that is so fine.

Samir Gohil (9)
Wanborough Primary School, Swindon

Puppy

P owerful and cute.
U ntidy, naughty.
P layful, stupid and adorable.
P inches food when he can.
Y awns when he's tired.

Liam Hobbs (8)
Wanborough Primary School, Swindon

The Rainbow

With the rain and the sun
Amazing rainbow made
With the colours dancing
With the raindrops gliding
With the colours leaping
With the sun beaming.

The blue is the sea
The green is the grass
The red is the flames
The yellow is the bee
All these colours make me grin
As they all sway with the wind.

With the gold jumping up and down
The indigos, the tree stands proud
With the orange as a pumpkin
And the violet is my pilot
The rainbow's pretty
And I feel witty.

Leanne Anderson (10)
Wanborough Primary School, Swindon

Animals Tanka

Horses are massive
Cats are small and cute, tiny
Dogs are big and play
Rabbits are very tiny
Pigs oink and it's annoying.

Charlotte Watson (8)
Wanborough Primary School, Swindon

The Beach Party

The music it sways away in the wind
And the food jumps out and says eat me
And the band plays their music
To the beat of the sun
The sound of the waves that channels the sea
And makes you happy.

The sand is as gold
As a Caribbean sunset
The sun umbrellas swirl with colour
Like spinning rainbows
This is so much fun
And the beat makes you run.

The sapphire sea whooshes
Like the washing machine turnin' the sea
You can sail the sea
You can surf the sea
But if you swallow too much
You will be churning, but we are only learnin'.

Oliver Herring (9)
Wanborough Primary School, Swindon

Footie

It is lots of fun.
Skills and amazing power.
Everyone cheering.
Football is for everyone.
The players want to score.

Fully packed with fans.
Everyone wants to win it.
Skills are amazing.
Everyone is scoring goals.
It's so important to them.

Oliver Cooke (9)
Wanborough Primary School, Swindon

Snow

When you make snow angels
Your legs and arms seem to flap like a bird
When you get up you can see the snow angel glisten like stars
The snow angel seems to come alive
The snow angel is speaking in a soft voice
Making a snow angel was a wonderful choice.

Snowball fights are the best
Even though the snow is a freezing cold ice lolly
And you could end up with a cold
It's still better than staying inside
Throwing snowballs is like throwing cotton wool
Having a snowball fight is extremely cool.

Making a snowman is really fun
The snowman comes alive, his arms jiggle in the wind
He has a big pebble grin
He has a human scarf and shiny human eyes
But when the sun comes out at the end of the day
The snowman melts away.

Thalia Gorvin (10)
Wanborough Primary School, Swindon

Yum-Yum Sweets

Sweets are more precious than big toys.
Sweets are like a big mouth-watering machine.
Sweets are more tastier than ice cream.
Sweets are very licky and very sticky.
Sweets are like jewels from a jewellery shop.
Sweets are yummy and very sugary and smooth.
Sweets are yummy and tasty.
Sweets make me very giddy and very jolly.

Elliot Street (7)
Wanborough Primary School, Swindon

One Night At The Fair

I headed for the candy,
then for the whammy bars,
I ate it all in one,
all in one night at the fair.

Then I saw the rollers,
I headed for The Loomer,
Then for the dodgems,
All in one night at the fair.

I saw my favourite game,
It is pin the tail on the donkey,
I asked if I could play,
All in one night at the fair.

Harry Chevis (8)
Wanborough Primary School, Swindon

Pippa My Pet

She's a rabbit,
Smooth, soft, small,
Scared of dogs,
Lawnmowers and balls.

She hops around,
In her silkish gown.

Bigger than her sisters,
Likes carrot tops.
Always friends
With cats, birds and wasps.

Dives into my mum's arms,
Always cuddly, sweet and calm.

Eleanor Rendell (8)
Wanborough Primary School, Swindon

My Favourite Things Haikus

Acting is my thing
Although I like singing too
Opera no way man.

Mr Guthrie's cool
Mr Guthrie has a ted
'Mr McTavage'.

Rachel Steven's sweet
Robbie Williams is great
But Girls Aloud top.

High heels bring it on
Dangle earrings are the style
Mini denim skirts.

Miss Clarke is lovely
Miss Clarke is as pretty as
A sparkling red rose.

Kate Winslet is great
Eddie Murphy is funny
Leonardo's fab.

Beatrice Nugent (8)
Wanborough Primary School, Swindon

Football

Man U are the best
Liverpool are a good team
Henry is rubbish
Van Nistelrooy rules
Wayne Rooney is very good
The Red Devils rule.

Sebastian Wylie (8)
Wanborough Primary School, Swindon

Hansel And Gretel

Hansel and Gretel,
What foolish kids,
Left a trail of bread and sticks,
Little Gretel cried and cried,
But an ugly witch spied and spied,
She made herself a gingerbread house,
The sweets would replace her ugly spouse,
The children ate like little pigs,
The witch grabbed them and smelt like figs,
Hansel was shoved in a cage,
A strange thing to do to a lad his age,
Gretel was set to work till dawn,
After a while she thought it a yawn,
And shoved the witch in the Aga,
Then sat with Hansel drinking lager!

Emily Spurdell (8)
Wanborough Primary School, Swindon

Who Am I? Haikus

Strong hands, good saver
Polish accent, bad thrower
Penalty saver.

Strong, flexible hands
Great goalie, humongous nose
Incredibly thin.

A sparkling goalie
Will entertain or bore you
Diving maniac.

Josh Reynolds (9)
Wanborough Primary School, Swindon

The Crown Jewels

I wandered into Buckingham Palace
In front of my eyes were the crown jewels
Glistening in the dark
The gems were calling straight to me
I could see the velvet cloak there in the distance
As the orb sprang out with a dance.

The black and white fur
Was a Dalmatian on a crown
The cross on the orb could never be timeless
Which almost blind me
The sceptre had quite a few gems
On its very long stem.

As it was time to go
I waved goodbye to the jewels
As they waved back
I walked out of the palace
When my face began to drown
But it was nice seeing the crown.

William Brittain (10)
Wanborough Primary School, Swindon

Chocolate Is . . .

Chocolate is as bad as a little brother,
Chocolate is as tasty as a bag of sweets,
Chocolate is bad for your teeth,
Chocolate is as yummy as toffee,
Chocolate is as crunchy as crisps,
Chocolate is as melty as snow!

James Warren (7)
Wanborough Primary School, Swindon

Music

Down the keys would gracefully step,
Imprisonment of the rhythm would plead freedom,
Bagpipes burst with expressive chords,
And the gentle hum of the cello would hum improvement
Hip hop keyboard will talk rhythm,
But the creatures in the instruments would never beg freedom.

Jazzy staccato would be guitar,
Deep sounds trying to trapeze your mind,
Snaky legato would soothe your body,
You can never find the right instrument,
Classical music will flow with calm,
So beautiful, enough to blow an alarm.

Piano is my music,
Swinging, swaying to the beat,
Eating up songs of amazement,
Played out through notes of Heaven,
Music makes you think you're dreaming
That it's only single meaning!

Luke Witts (10)
Wanborough Primary School, Swindon

Sweets

Sweets are yummy
Sweets are awesomely tasty
Sweets are colourful

Sweets are wonderful
Sweets are different colours
Sweets are brilliant

Sweets are so dreamy
Too many are unhealthy
I love awesome sweets.

Ryan Bunce (9)
Wanborough Primary School, Swindon

Chocolate

Chocolate is very sweet
Chocolate is like having a birthday
Chocolate is making my mouth water
Chocolate is sugary
Chocolate makes me feel sick
Chocolate is very sticky
Chocolate is like my best dream ever.

Thomas Spackman (8)
Wanborough Primary School, Swindon

Spain

The bright bulging lights of the wacky funfairs
And the crazy, colossal roller coasters
Gorgeous hot summer day and cool winter breezes
The happiness goes on
The sparkling light blue sea glistening in the sunlight
The sun sparkles in the sky like a diamond.

Indya Grand (9)
Wanborough Primary School, Swindon

My Favourite Things

F amilies can be small, mine is huge!
A nimals fascinate me.
V ery often I'm alone
O n my own,
U p on my bed I read my books
R eading, reading and reading.
I also love smiling babies
T ogether these mean so much to me
E verlasting they will be.

Bethany Williams (10)
Westlea Primary School, Swindon

My Guinea Pig

G ot to eat
U nlike others
I 'm very greedy
N ice and cuddly
E very day
A nice pet

P laying around
I like to run
G lorious guinea pigs.

Gordon Wai (8)
Westlea Primary School, Swindon

Family

F antastic families
A re always there for me.
M y family is very special to me.
I f they care for me I will care for them.
L oving them is something I will always do.
Y our family loves you too.

Sophie Peart (8)
Westlea Primary School, Swindon

Great Guitars

Guitars are great,
They are just like a mate,
Though the frets are hard to press,
Guitars are the best,
Rock music is what some are used to playing,
I like playing the guitar every day!

Tess Pringle (8)
Westlea Primary School, Swindon

Rap Dog

My dog was in the cloakroom, he was taking his time
When slowly the door opened and out he started to climb
He was wearing my hoody and he had earphones on
He had flashy trainers and a cool rap song!

Hey little people I'm the proper Snoop Dog
And in my Mercedes I'm a dog road hog
You might have heard a rumour that I'm scared of cats
But if you're very clever you won't believe that.

You should all know I'm the master of bling
Actually come to think of it I'm the king
If you need to call me I have a name
Rap Dog is how I have earned my fame!

Hannah Sharp (10)
Westlea Primary School, Swindon

Feet!

Feet, feet, good to meet
Cats wandering the street with their feet,
But they are not very tasty to eat!

If someone cheats,
You can get to your feet,
And not care a bit about sleet!

Make sure you don't stand
On any parakeets with your feet,
And tap your toes to the beat!

Be neat with your feet,
Don't stand on your seat
And don't greet with your feet!
Feet!

Elijah Begen (7)
Whitehall Primary School, Bristol

If I Was From America . . .

If I was from America
I'd sit and watch myself on TV,
I'd go to shopping malls every day
Because a film star always needs new clothes.
I might go and live in Kansas,
As my friend Dorothy says it's nice over there,
'There's no place like home,' she says.
But I'd be careful of twisters.
My car would be a huge limo
That I would drive around in all the time,
Except when I was riding my horse.
I'd be a film star like Indiana Jones.
I'd work in Hollywood!
My accent would be wonderful
Like Disney's Mickey Mouse.
I would visit the White House every day
And send letters of complaint to the President.
I'd always carry a mobile phone
To text my pals with.
But I would never accept a gun
Because guns kill.

Martha Hayes (8)
Whitehall Primary School, Bristol

S Is For School

S is for school where we all go to learn
C is for conversation that we all have at school
H is for history, that is one of the lessons we do at school
O is for organise, the teachers do before lessons start.
O is for office where we all go when we are late for school.
L is for listening to what we all have to in lessons.

Chantelle-Rose Clarke
Whitehall Primary School, Bristol

The Kid Skater

There was a kid skater
Who said, 'See you later!'
He thought he was cool
But just was a fool.

He skated so badly
And cried home so sadly.
His mum said, 'No . . .'
But he said, 'So!'

He fell off one day
In an awkward way.
He grazed his knee
And got stung by a bee.

He made a friend
And finally got round the bend.
They skate every day
In a happy way.

Chloe Nicholls (10)
Whitehall Primary School, Bristol

My Pet Laddie

My dog's name is Laddie.
He thinks he is a baddie.
He guards my house
Even from a mouse.

He started to chase
And won the race.
He fell over a log
And got lost in the fog.

He found his way out
And he was out and about.
He was back home
And he was home alone.

Nathan Fuller (9)
Whitehall Primary School, Bristol

My House Has Been Taken Over!

My house has been taken over
You can't guess what's within,
Piles of clothes coming in droves
I really just can't win!

My house has been taken over
There is a dragon down the loo,
Teachers in the bathroom
And the head is in there too!

My house has been taken over
There are ants swarming on my floor,
And in my bed, a fish called Ted
Oh it wasn't like this before!

My house has been taken over
There are termites in my shoe,
A crazy hamster in the kitchen
And a hopping mad kangaroo!

My house has been taken over
I don't know how or when,
But I'll very soon get very fed up
I hope they'll go home again!

Flora Begen (11)
Whitehall Primary School, Bristol